In the Shade of His Names

A Journey from Collapse to Clarity

Dr. Ashi Ezz

Copyright © 2025 by Dr. Ashi Ezz

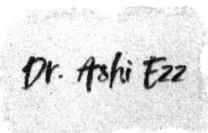

Thank you for purchasing an authorized edition of this book. Copyright fuels creativity, encourages diverse voices, promotes free speech, and contributes to a vibrant culture. By complying with copyright laws and not reproducing, scanning, or distributing any part of this book in any form without permission, you are supporting writers and allowing the continuation of publishing works for every reader.

First edition

Paperback ISBN: 978-1-0670520-8-9

Kindle & EPUB ISBN: 978-1-0670520-9-6

While the author has made every effort to provide accurate Internet addresses at the time of publication, neither the author nor the publisher assumes any responsibility for errors or changes that occur after publication. The author also does not have any control over and does not assume any responsibility for third-party websites or their content.

For inquiries, further information, please contact:

Email: ashiezzpublish@gmail.com

Dedication

In the name of our Lord, the Creator of all, though many walk blind to see the truth's call. It's not the eyes that fail to see, but the hearts that lose its way.

And know that there is no goodness in any good that is followed by the Fire (of Hell), and there is no evil in any action that is followed by Paradise.

To the Seeker whose heart is a vessel of longing, whose soul is a mirror yearning to reflect the Divine;

This book is a garden where the Names of Allah bloom, every Name is a door, every letter a key. Step forward with trembling hands and open the gates of light.

I dedicate this book to those whose hearts are thirsty for meaning, whose souls seek refuge in the vastness of Allah's Names. May each Name be a drop of mercy upon your tongue, a whisper of peace in your prayers, a lantern guiding you home.

Declaration

Always turn to the Quran and authentic Hadith; their light reveals the truth. Any comparisons, metaphors, or imagery in this book are only tools to simplify complex ideas, never reflections of God's true essence.

As the Quran reminds us:

"There is nothing like Him" (Ash-Shura 42:11),

"To Him belongs the highest example" (An-Nahl 16:60).

God is beyond all likeness, and His reality is beyond human grasp. If truth shines through these words, it is by His mercy. If there are flaws, they are mine alone.

Allah is perfect.

His Messenger is pure.

Contents

Introduction 1

Allah (The One True God) 14

1. Ar-Rahman الرَّحْمَنُ (The Most Gracious) 17

2. Ar-Rahim الرَّحِيمُ (The Most Merciful) 19

3. Al-Malik المَلِكُ (The King and Owner of Dominion) 20

4. Al-Quddus القُدُّوسُ (The Absolutely Pure and Holy) 22

5. As-Salam السَّلَامُ (The Source of Peace and Safety) 24

6. Al-Mu'min المُؤْمِنُ (The Giver of Faith and Security) 26

7. Al-Muhaymin المُهَيْمِنُ (The All-Controlling) 27

8. Al-Aziz العَزِيزُ (The Almighty) 29

9. Al-Jabbar الجَبَّارُ (The Compeller) 31

10. Al-Mutakabbir المُتَكَبِّرُ (The Supreme) 33

11. Al-Khaliq الخَالِقُ (The Creator) 35

12. Al-Bari البَارِئُ (The Evolver) 37

13. Al-Musawwir المُصَوِّرُ (The Fashioner) 38

14. Al-Ghaffar الغَفَّارُ (The Constant Forgiver) 40

15. Al-Qahhar القَهَّارُ (The All-Prevailing One) 42

16. Al-Wahhab الوَهَّابُ (The Supreme Bestower) 43

17. Ar-Razzaq الرَّزَّاقُ (The Provider) 45

18. Al-Fattah الفَتَّاحُ (The Supreme Solver) 47

19. Al-'Alim العَلِيمُ (The All-Knowing) 49

20. Al-Qabid القَابِضُ (The Withholder) 50

21. Al-Basit البَاسِطُ (The Extender) 52

22. Al-Khafid الخَافِضُ (The Reducer) 54

23. Ar-Rafi الرَّافِعُ (The Exalter)....................................... 56

24. Al-Mu'izz المُعِزُّ (The Honourer-Bestower) 57

25. Al-Mudhill المُذِلُّ (The Dishonourer)............................. 59

26. As-Sami السَّمِيعُ (The All-Hearing) 61

27. Al-Basir البَصِيرُ (The All-Seeing) 63

28. Al-Hakam الحَكَمُ (The Impartial Judge) 64

29. Al-'Adl العَدْلُ (The Just One) 66

30. Al-Latif اللَّطِيفُ (The Subtle One)................................... 68

31. Al-Khabir الخَبِيرُ (The All-Aware) 70

32. Al-Halim الحَلِيمُ (The Most Forbearing)......................... 72

33. Al-'Azim العَظِيمُ (The Magnificent) 74

34. Al-Ghaffur الغَفُورُ (The Great Forgiver)......................... 75

35. Ash-Shakur الشَّكُورُ (The Most Appreciative) 77

36. Al-'Aliyy العَلِيُّ (The Most High, The Exalted)................. 79

37. Al-Kabir الكَبِيرُ (The Most Great) 81

38. Al-Hafiz الحَفِيظُ (The Preserver).................................... 83

39. Al-Muqit المُقِيتُ (The Sustainer) 85

40. Al-Hasib الحَسِيبُ (The Reckoner) 87

41. Al-Jalil الجَلِيلُ (The Majestic)....................................... 89

42. Al-Karim الكَرِيمُ (The Most Generous, The Most Esteemed) 91

43. Ar-Raqib الرَّقِيبُ (The Watchful) 92

44. Al-Mujib المُجِيبُ (The Responsive One) 93

45. Al-Wasi' الوَاسِعُ (The All-Encompassing, The Boundless) 94
46. Al-Hakim الحَكِيمُ (The All-Wise) 96
47. Al-Wadud الوَدُودُ (The Most Loving) 97
48. Al-Majid المَجِيدُ (The Glorious, The Most Honorable) 99
49. Al-Ba'ith البَاعِثُ (The Infuser of New Life) 101
50. Ash-Shahid الشَّهِيدُ (The All-and-Ever Witnessing) 103
51. Al-Haqq الحَقُّ (The Absolute Truth) 105
52. Al-Wakil الوَكِيلُ (The Trustee) 107
53. Al-Qawiyy القَوِيُّ (The All-Strong) 109
54. Al-Matin المَتِينُ (The Firm One) 110
55. Al-Wali الوَلِيُّ (The Protector) 111
56. Al-Hamid الحَمِيدُ (The Most Praiseworthy) 113
57. Al-Muhsi المُحْصِي (The All-Enumerating, The Counter) 115
58. Al-Mubdi المُبْدِئُ (The Originator, The Initiator) 117
59. Al-Mu'id المُعِيدُ (The Restorer, The Reinstater) 119
60. Al-Muhyi المُحْيِي (The Giver of Life) 121
61. Al-Mumit المُمِيتُ (The Creator of Death) 123
62. Al-Hayy الحَيُّ (The Ever-Living) 125
63. Al-Qayyum القَيُّومُ (The Sustainer, The Self-Subsisting) 127
64. Al-Wajid الوَاجِدُ (The Perceiver) 129
65. Al-Majid المَاجِدُ (The Glorious, Most Honorable) 131
66. Al-Wahid الوَاحِدُ (The Only One) 133

67. Al-Ahad الأَحَدُ (The Indivisible, The One) 134

68. As-Samad الصَّمَدُ (The Self-Sufficient, The Impregnable) 135

69. Al-Qadir القَادِرُ (The Omnipotent) 137

70. Al-Muqtadir المُقْتَدِرُ (The Creator of All Power) 139

71. Al-Muqaddim المُقَدِّمُ (The Expediter) 141

72. Al-Mu'akhkhir المُؤَخِّرُ (The Delayer) 143

73. Al-Awwal الأَوَّلُ (The First) 145

74. Al-Akhir الآخِرُ (The Last) 147

75. Az-Zahir الظَّاهِرُ (The Manifest) 148

76. Al-Batin البَاطِنُ (The Hidden One, Knower of the Hidden) 149

77. Al-Waali الوَالِي (The Sole Governor) 150

78. Al-Muta'ali المُتَعَالِي (The Self-Exalted) 151

79. Al-Barr البَرُّ (The Source of All Goodness) 152

80. At-Tawwab التَّوَّابُ (The Ever-Pardoning) 153

81. Al-Muntaqim المُنْتَقِمُ (The Just Requitor) 156

82. Al-'Afuww العَفُوُّ (The Supreme Pardoner) 158

83. Ar-Ra'uf الرَّءُوفُ (The Most Kind) 160

84. Malik-ul-Mulk مَالِكُ المُلْكِ (Master of the Kingdom, Owner of the Dominion) 162

85. Dhul-Jalali Wal-Ikram ذُو الجَلَالِ وَالإِكْرَامِ (Possessor of Glory and Honor) 164

86. Al-Muqsit المُقْسِطُ (The Just One) 166

87. Al-Jami' الجَامِعُ (The Gatherer, the Uniter) 168

88. Al-Ghaniyy الغَنِيُّ (The Self-Sufficient, the Wealthy) 170

89. Al-Mughni المُغْنِي (The Enricher) 172

90. Al-Mani' المَانِعُ (The Withholder)................................. 174

91. Ad-Darr الضَّارُّ (The Distresser)................................... 176

92. An-Nafi' النَّافِعُ (The Propitious, the Benefactor)........... 178

93. An-Nur النُّورُ (The Light) 181

94. Al-Hadi الهَادِي (The Guide)... 183

95. Al-Badi البَدِيعُ (Incomparable Originator)..................... 185

96. Al-Baqi البَاقِي (The Ever-Surviving)............................. 187

97. Al-Warith الوَارِثُ (The Inheritor) 189

98. As-Sabur الصَّبُورُ (The Forbearing)............................... 191

99. Ar-Rashid الرَّشِيدُ (The Guide, Infallible Teacher, and Knower) 193

Epilogue 196

The Book Cover... 230

Acknowledgments... 231

References.. 232

About the Author 234

Introduction

In the name of the Beloved, the All-Merciful, the All-Knowing. Let us embark on a journey, not of mere words, but of the heart, to uncover the luminous tapestry of Allah's Names and Attributes. For this is no ordinary study; it is a light of the soul, calling us to know Him, to love Him, and to reflect His light in our lives.

Why I Write This Book

This book was born from a yearning; **not just to know Allah**, but to **live through His Names**. His Names are more than theology; they are divine tools, offered to us for navigating the complexities of life through His grace and mercy.

Allah did not reveal His Beautiful Names for passive learning alone. it is an **invitation** to **reflect**, to **embody**, and to **transform**.

And the reason runs even deeper.

In the Qur'an, Allah says:

"And [mention, O Muhammad], when your Lord said to the angels, 'Indeed, I will make upon the earth a successive authority (khalīfah).' They said, 'Will You place upon it one who causes corruption therein and sheds blood, while we declare Your praise and

sanctify You?' Allah said, 'Indeed, I know that which you do not know.'"
; *Surah Al-Baqarah (2:30)*

Here, Allah announces that He will place a **khalifah**; a vicegerent, a steward; on Earth. That steward is the human being. And with that divine role comes a sacred trust: **to reflect Allah's Names and Attributes in our conduct**; not because we are divine, but because we are called to **mirror divine qualities** in how we lead, love, decide, and heal.

Ar-Raheem calls us to show mercy in our relationships. *Al-Adl* inspires us to stand for justice. *As-Saboor* teaches us endurance through trials. *Al-Ghafoor* invites us to forgive as we wish to be forgiven. Each Name becomes a compass, pointing us to **what it truly means to be Allah's representative on Earth**.

This book is about helping us become more grounded, more conscious, and more resilient. By exploring the Names of Allah, supported by hadith that reflect their meanings, and practical reflections for daily life, we aim to reach a deeper purpose. That's why, with each Name, I've included wisdom from our beloved Prophet wherever it fits; to help us not only nourish our hearts but also strengthen our role as khalifah on Earth. It's a way to become guiding lights in a world that often forgets its true Source.

The Essence of Allah's Names and Attributes

To speak of Allah's Names and Attributes is to speak of the ocean while standing at its shore. The Names

(Asma') are the waves that crash upon the heart, each one a revelation of His beauty and majesty. The Attributes (Sifat) are the depths beneath, the unseen currents that carry the essence of His being. Together, they are the bridge between the Creator and the created, a path for the seeker to draw nearer to the Divine.

The Quran, that eternal love letter, calls out:
"To Allah belong the Most Beautiful Names, so call upon Him by them." (Surah Al-A'raf 7:180)
And the Prophet Muhammad (peace be upon him), the guide of believers, said:
"Allah has ninety-nine Names, one hundred minus one; whoever memorizes them will enter Paradise." (Sahih Bukhari & Muslim)

The breath of Names and Attributes

What is the difference between a Name and an Attribute? Let me introduce you to the best of what I learn about that throughout my reading: the Name express the being of the Divine, while the Attribute is the breath behind it.

- The Name *Allah* is the essence, the purest reflection of His being. It is the sun that illuminates all other Names.

- The Attribute like *Ar-Rahman* (The Most Merciful) is the warmth of that sun, the tenderness that embraces all creation.

Every Name carries an Attribute, but not every Attribute is a Name. For example, *Mercy* (Rahma) is an Attribute, but *Ar-Rahman* is both a Name and an Attribute. Why? Because it has reached the pinnacle of perfection, a perfection that belongs only to Him.

The Three Faces of Divine Names

The Names of Allah are like a garden, each flower blooming with its own fragrance. They can be divided into three categories:

1. **Names of Majesty (Jalal):** These are like the thunder and the lightning, the awe-inspiring power of the Divine.
    - *Al-Jabbar* (The Compeller)
    - *Al-Mutakabbir* (The Supreme)
    - *Dhu Al-Jalali wal-Ikram* (Possessor of Glory and Honor)

These Names remind us of His greatness, His sovereignty over all that exists. They humble us, bringing us to our knees in reverence.

2. **Names of Beauty (Jamal):** These are like the gentle rain, the soft breeze, the mercy that sustains all life.
    - *Ar-Rahman* (The Most Merciful)
    - *Ar-Rahim* (The Most Compassionate)
    - *Al-Wadud* (The Loving)

These Names call us to embody His mercy, to be vessels of His love in this world.

3. **Names of Perfection (Kamal):** These are the eternal truths, the unchanging essence of the Divine.
    - *Al-Hayy* (The Ever-Living)
    - *Al-Qayyum* (The Self-Sustaining)
    - *Al-Ahad* (The One)

These Names remind us that He is beyond time, beyond need, beyond comparison.

The Attributes: A Mirror of Divine Action

The Attributes of Allah are like the movements of His hand in the world. They are divided into three:

1. **Essential Attributes (Sifat Dhatiyah):** These are the qualities that define His very essence.
    - *Al-Wujud* (Existence)
    - *Al-Qidam* (Eternality)

These Attributes are the unshakable truths that define Him.

2. **Attributes of Action (Sifat Al-Af'al):** These are the acts of creation, provision, and sustenance.
    - *Al-Khaliq* (The Creator)
    - *Al-Razzaq* (The Provider)

These Attributes remind us that every breath, every morsel of food, every moment of life is a gift from Him.

3. **Negative Attributes (Sifat Salbiyyah):** the qualities He is free from.

- *Al-Awwal* (The First) – He has no beginning.
- *Al-Akhir* (The Last) – He has no end.

These Attributes remind us of His transcendence, His absolute independence from all creation.

The Seeker's Path

To know Allah's Names and Attributes is not to memorize a list, but to let them transform you. When you call upon *Ar-Rahman*, let His mercy flow through you to others. When you reflect on *Al-Jabbar*, let His strength guide you through trials. When you whisper *Al-Wadud*, let His love fill your heart.

Adopt the character traits of His names
This is the ultimate goal: to become a mirror, reflecting His light in the world.

Why Allah's Names Matter

Allah says in the Quran:
"And to Allah belong the best names, so invoke Him by them." (Quran 7:180)
Can you hear it? The call of the Divine, echoing through the heavens and the earth, inviting us to know Him through His names. These names are **keys to the heart of the universe**, doors to His mercy,

and pathways to His love. When you call upon **Ar-Rahman (The Most Merciful),** you are not just uttering a name; you are invoking the boundless mercy that cradles creation. When you whisper **Al-Quddus (The Holy)**, you are touching the purity that transcends all imperfections.

Why do these names matter? Because they are the **essence of our faith**, the light that guides us through the darkness of this world. They remind us that Allah is not distant; He is **Al-Qareeb (The Near)**, closer to us than our jugular vein. They teach us that He is **As-Salam (The Source of Peace)**, the One who can calm the storms within us.

The Gifts of Knowing Allah's Names

When you truly know Allah's names, your heart begins to jump with joy, your soul finds its anchor, and your life transforms. Let me tell you about the gifts that come with this knowledge:

a. The Gift of Unshakable Faith

When you know that Allah is **Ar-Razzaq (The Provider)**, you no longer fear poverty. You understand that your sustenance flows from His infinite bounty. When you know He is **Al-Hakim (The Wise)**, you trust His plan, even when life feels uncertain. Faith becomes your fortress, unshakable and eternal.

b. The Gift of Answered Prayers

The Prophet (peace be upon him) taught us to call upon Allah using His beautiful names. Imagine standing before Him, your heart trembling with hope, and you say: *"Ya Ghaffar, forgive me. Ya Razzaq, provide for me."* These names are not just words; they are **divine invitations**, promises that He will answer.

c. The Gift of a Pure Heart

When you know Allah is **Al-Qawiyy (The Strong)** and **Al-Aziz (The Almighty)**, your heart is freed from the chains of fear. You no longer tremble before the power of creation, for you know that all power belongs to Him. Your heart becomes a sanctuary of peace, untouched by the chaos of the world.

Nevertheless, in our journey to know Allah's names, we must tread carefully, avoiding pitfalls and ask ourselves some questions:

Are Allah's Names Limited to 99?

Some scholars believe that Allah has 99 names, while others see this as only a glimpse of a much deeper reality. In my view, the hadith mentioning 99 names does not restrict Allah's names to that number. Rather, it highlights a special set of names with distinct virtues. The rest remain part of the unseen; known only to Him.

Think of the 99 names as stars in the night sky: guiding lights on our journey. Yet beyond these stars lies an infinite universe of divine attributes that only Allah fully comprehends.

The Prophet (peace be upon him) beautifully expressed this reality when he said:
"I cannot praise You as You deserve. You are as You have praised Yourself."
(*Sahih Muslim*)

This hadith reminds us that no matter how much we know or how deeply we reflect, we can never fully grasp the greatness of Allah. The 99 names are not a limit but an invitation; a divine gift that opens the door to knowing Him.

Dear seeker, know this: the names of Allah known to creation are not confined to ninety-nine. They are as limitless as His mercy and as vast as His wisdom.

Each name is a doorway to a world of meaning, waiting to be explored.

Throughout Islamic history, scholars; both classical and contemporary; have engaged in meaningful debate over the identification of these names. Some insist on restricting them to those explicitly found in the Qur'an and Sunnah, while others draw from deeper interpretations of sacred texts. This scholarly pursuit has been both noble and enduring.

For the purpose of this book, I dwell upon names renowned and widely known, not to diminish the depths of study but to embrace what remains shrouded, unknowable. Had Allah willed a list complete and clear, His wisdom would have revealed it; perfect, bright, sincere.

There is wisdom in this ambiguity. It encourages reflection, seeking, and learning. The more we search for His names, the more we come to know our Lord. As the Qur'an reminds us:
"Allah does not burden a soul beyond what it can bear."
(*Surah Al-Baqarah, 2:286*)

And so, I humbly present the names most familiar to us, fully aware that they point to a divine reality far greater; one known only to Him.

Can We Invent Names for Allah?

Based on what I've read and what sits right in my heart; no, we cannot. Allah's names are established through the Qur'an and authentic Sunnah. For example, we shouldn't call Him *"Al-Mudabbir"* (The Planner) just because He plans. His names are divine and not open to personal invention.

However, some scholars have derived names from the meanings of certain verses or hadiths. While these may reflect attributes of Allah, they remain interpretative. We may refer to them descriptively, but we cannot confirm them as official names unless explicitly stated in revelation.

I have done my best to compile them thoughtfully. Still, full confirmation of the exact 99 names rests with Allah alone and will only be known when He chooses to reveal them with certainty.

Can We Use His Names for Creation?

Some names, like **Ar-Raheem (The Merciful)**, can describe humans in a limited sense. But names like **Al-Khaliq (The Creator)** are exclusive to Allah. This distinction preserves His majesty.

The Pillars of Belief in Allah's Names

To truly understand Allah's names, we must build our belief on three pillars:

a. Believe in the Name

We must accept every name of Allah as it is revealed. For example, we must believe that He is **Al-Malik (The King)** and **Al-Jabbar (The Compeller)**.

b. Believe in the Meaning

Each name carries a universe of meaning. **Al-Hakeem (The Wise)** means His wisdom is perfect, encompassing all things. **Al-Ghaffar (The Forgiver)** means His mercy is vast, ready to embrace the repentant soul.

c. Believe in the Effects

These names are not just words; they have power. When you call upon **Al-Mujeeb (The Responsive)**, you are calling upon the One who answers. When you seek refuge in **As-Salam (The Source of Peace)**, you are seeking the One who brings tranquility to your heart.

Living with Allah's Names

Knowing Allah's names is not just an act of worship; it is a way of life. When you feel weak, remember He is **Al-Qawiyy (The Strong)**. When you feel lost, remember He is **Al-Hadi (The Guide)**. When you feel alone, remember He is **Al-Wali (The Protector)**. These names are not just for recitation; they are for **transformation**. They are the light that guides us, the strength that sustains us, and the love that fills us.

The Journey Begins

Dear reader, the journey to know Allah's names is a journey to know yourself, to know your Creator, and to find your purpose.

Let this be your starting point. Let His names be your companions, your guides, and your solace. For in His names, you will find everything you seek: **peace, love, and the eternal embrace of your Lord.**

May Allah guide us to understand His beautiful names and live by their meanings. Ameen.

Allah (The One True God)

The name "Allah" is mentioned 2,699 times in the Qur'an. This includes different grammatical forms such as (Allah), (Allah in genitive case), and (Allahumma - O Allah).

Key Verses: *Mentioned in 2:255, 3:18, 20:8, and throughout the Qur'an*

Let us begin with the Name that carries the weight of the universe and the light of eternity; **Allah.** *Not merely a word, but the very pulse of existence, the breath of life, the essence of all that is.*

"Allah – there is no deity except Him. To Him belong the best names." *(Quran 20:8)*

To call upon Allah is to summon **Al-Hayy** *(The Ever-Living),* **Al-Qayyum** *(The Self-Sustaining),* **Ar-Rahman** *(The Most Merciful).*

His Name is not bound by time or place; it is a refuge for the lost, a sanctuary for the weary, a light in the depths of darkness.

"Do you know of any namesake for Him?" *(Quran 19:65)*

O seeker, when you whisper Allah, know that He is closer than your own breath, nearer than the unspoken prayers hidden in your heart. His Name is a gateway to mercy, a key to love, a path to forgiveness. It is singular, for He is **Al-Wahid** (The One), **Al-Ahad** (The Unique), beyond all comparison:

"Say, He is Allah, the One. Allah, the Eternal Refuge. He neither begets nor is born, nor is there to Him any equivalent." (Quran 112:1-4)

This Name is not just spoken; it is felt. It flows not from the tongue alone but from the soul. Even its letters rest within the tongue, a secret between you and your Lord.

No eyes have seen Him by the light of sight, but hearts have known Him in faith's pure light.
No mind can grasp Him through thought or sense, nor likeness draw His true essence.
By signs He's known, by truths revealed, in every mark, His name is sealed.

Let it awaken your heart at dawn, and when the weight of the world presses upon you, let it revive you once more. The Prophet (SAW) said:

"The example of the one who remembers his Lord and the one who does not is like the example of the living and the dead." (Sahih Bukhari)

The moon is one, yet its reflections are many. So too is **Allah,** and to Him belongs the highest example; the One reflected in the hearts of His creation. His Name gathers all His Divine Names; **Ar-Rahman,**

Al-Qadir, Al-Ghaffar; yet remains One in Essence, One in Power, One in Mercy.

Let His Name be your companion in the morning and your solace in the night. Let it remind you of His greatness as the stars remind you of His vastness. The Prophet (SAW) said:

"The best remembrance is to say: La ilaha illallah (There is no god but Allah)." *(Sunan At-Tirmidhi)*

The Prophet Muhammad (peace be upon him) said that Allah said to Musa (Moses, peace be upon him):

"O Musa, if the seven heavens and all that they contain besides Me, and the seven earths as well, were placed in one side of the scale, and La ilaha illa Allah (There is no deity worthy of worship except Allah) was placed on the other side, the latter would outweigh them all." Ibn Hibban in his Sahih (Hadith 8157).

O Allah, Awaken our souls with Your remembrance, and let Your Name be the light that guides us through every storm.

"Allah is the Light of the heavens and the earth." *(Quran 24:35)*

May we live in awe of You, die in love with You, and be resurrected in Your mercy. **Ameen.**

"Indeed, in the remembrance of Allah do hearts find rest." *(Quran 13:28)*

1. Ar-Rahman الرَّحْمَنُ (The Most Gracious)

---

*The name "**Ar-Rahman**" is mentioned 57 times in the Qur'an.*

***Key Verses**: Mentioned in 1:1, 19:58, 20:5, 55:1*

---

*Mercy, boundless, unfathomable, embracing all. He is **Ar-Rahman**, whose mercy encompasses all creation, and **Ar-Raheem**, whose mercy is specially reserved for the believers.*

"And My mercy encompasses all things."
(Quran 7:156)

He forgives the sinner, answers the supplicant, and grants paradise to those who seek Him. Even a mother's love for her child is but a fraction of His infinite compassion.

He who gives before you ask, who nurtures before you know need.

The sun does not choose whom it warms, nor does the rain ask where to fall.

Love flows from Him to all creation, without measure, without condition.

If you saw how He cares for you, even in your forgetfulness, your heart would melt in gratitude.

What mercy is this, that the one who turns away is still invited back?

His grace is not earned, it is given; breathe it in, for it surrounds you.

To see Ar-Rahman, look at the mother feeding her child, the tree shading the weary traveler, the stranger who smiles without reason.

Let your kindness mirror His, and your soul will know peace.

"The believers are like one body; if one part suffers, the whole body responds with sleeplessness and fever."
Sahih Muslim

2. Ar-Rahim الرَّحِيمُ (The Most Merciful)

The Most Merciful is mentioned 114 times in the Qur'an.

Key Verses: *Mentioned in 1:1, 2:163, 3:31, 5:98, 12:64*

Mercy is the bridge between your fall and your rise.
He does not count your slips; He counts your steps back to Him.
A tear of regret is dearer to Him than a thousand words of pride.
You fear your sins, yet He has already prepared their forgiveness.
The door of mercy is never closed, only hearts close themselves to it.
To wrong yourself is human, but to despair in His mercy is blindness.
Every dawn is a whisper: "Come back, and your Lord will embrace you again."
The farther you have wandered, the greater His joy at your return.

"None of you will enter Paradise until you have faith, and none of you truly have faith until you love each other."
Sahih Muslim

3. Al-Malik الْمَلِكُ (The King and Owner of Dominion)

The name "Al-Malik" The King, The Absolute Ruler is mentioned 5 times in the Qur'an.

Key Verses: *Mentioned in 59:23, 20:114*

"So exalted is Allah, the Sovereign, the Truth; there is no deity except Him, Lord of the Noble Throne." *Surah Al-Mu'minun (23:116)*

The world is but a shadow of His majesty, yet He governs it with gentleness.

Kings rule with limit power, but He rules with omnipotence.

To Him belongs the seen and the unseen, the past and what is yet to be.

Kings build kingdoms; He builds hearts.

Just remember and don't be delusion

Al-Mālik, Owner of all things,

To Him belong both slaves and kings.

What we possess is but on loan,

Returned the day we journey home.

They claim with pride, "This land is mine,"

A fleeting voice in borrowed time.

Yet dust they were, and dust remain;

What can they own that won't decay?

You own nothing, yet He allows you to carry His gifts; be grateful.

The one who bows to Al-Malik walks upright before all others.

What you seek in the world, He holds in abundance; turn to the King of kings.

"He who humbles himself for Allah, Allah will raise him."
Sahih Muslim

4. Al-Quddus القُدُّوسُ (The Absolutely Pure and Holy)

The name "Al-Quddus" The Absolutely Pure and Holy is mentioned two times in the Qur'an.

Key Verses: *Mentioned in 59:23, 62:1*

"Whatever is in the heavens and whatever is on the earth is exalting Allah, the Sovereign, the Pure, the Exalted in Might, the Wise."
Surah Al-Jumu'ah (62:1)

Al-Quddus, Holy, vast, and high,

Above the earth, beyond the sky.

No thought can grasp, no eye can see,

The One who was and still shall be.

He needs no throne, no food, no rest,

Perfection robed in Holiness.

He is the light untouched by shadow, the truth untainted by doubt.

His purity is not only in being, but in giving; every soul longs to return to Him.

The one who seeks Al-Quddus must cleanse not only bodies, but heart and souls.

Be as the river that purifies itself as it flows, always seeking the ocean.

Let go of what corrupts you, and you will find yourself drawn to Him.

No impurity can touch Him, yet He welcomes the impure who seek cleansing.

When the heart is washed in remembrance, it reflects His perfection.

5. As-Salam السَّلَامُ (The Source of Peace and Safety)

As-Salām" The Source of Peace and Safety is mentioned once in the Qur'an.

Key Verses: *Mentioned in Surah Al-Hashr (59:23)*

The restless heart finds no home but in Him.

Peace is not the absence of struggle, but the presence of As-Salam within.

Winds may roar and waves may rise, but the one anchored in Him is unshaken.

The world promises peace but delivers only distraction.

As-Salam is not found in the silence of the world, but in the peace of the soul.

Surrender to Him, and the storm inside you will settle.

He teaches us how to walk in peace with others:

'And when the ignorant address them with harsh words, they respond with peace.'

(Surah Al-Furqan, 25:63)

Such are the 'servants of the Most Merciful', marked by wisdom and humility.

When met with ignorance or hostility, they rise above anger, reply with grace, and part ways in peace.

"He who believes in Allah and the Last Day should not harm his neighbor."
Sahih Bukhari

6. Al-Mu'min المُؤْمِنُ (The Giver of Faith and Security)

The name "Al-Mu'min" The Giver of Faith and Security is mentioned once in the Qur'an.

Key Verses: *Mentioned in Surah Al-Hashr (59:23)*

Faith is not knowing the path, but trusting the Guide.

When the world is a storm, faith is the ship that does not sink.

To believe is to walk into darkness and know there is light ahead.

Faith is not built in comfort but in the fire of trial.

The one who leans on Al-Mu'min will never be abandoned.

Security is not in wealth, nor in power, but in the certainty of His presence.

Close your eyes and leap towards his light; the peace will catch you.

"Whoever guides someone to goodness will have a reward like one who did it."
Sahih Muslim

7. Al-Muhaymin اَلْمُهَيْمِنُ (The All-Controlling)

The name "Al-Muhaymin" The All-Controlling/The Guardian is mentioned once in the Qur'an.

Key Verses: *Mentioned in Surah Al-Hashr (59:23)*

You do not see Him, yet He watches over you.

He guarded you before you knew you needed guarding.

"And they did not estimate Allah with true estimation," *Surah Al-Anbiya (21:66)*

His power and majesty they failed to see,

The earth in His grip, the heavens too,

Yet they deny the One, whose might is true.

You are never alone; His care surrounds you like the unseen air.

Birds do not store their food, yet they sleep in peace; why do you worry?

He who watches over the stars will not forget a single heart that calls on Him.

Even in your lowest moment, He is closer to you than your own soul.

If you knew how much He protects you from, you would fall in gratitude.

"He who relieves a hardship for a believer in this world, Allah will relieve a hardship for him on the Day of Judgment."
Sahih Muslim

8. Al-Aziz العَزِيزُ (The Almighty)

The name "Al-'Aziz" The Almighty is mentioned 92 times in the Qur'an.

Key Verses: Mentioned in 3:6, 4:158, 59:23

True strength does not come from the sword, nor from wealth, nor from the fleeting praise of men.

*It comes from **Al-Aziz**, the Mighty One, whose throne is above all thrones, whose decree none can overturn.*

He is the source of honor; so why seek validation from the transient, when the Eternal calls you to Him?

"Allah is Exalted in Might and Wise."

(Quran 2:209)

In His hands, the heavens and the earth lie,

The Sovereign One who makes it grow,

Yet many still refuse to know.

Power is His alone; yet He gives strength to the weak.

The mountains bow before Him, yet He listens to the whisper of the broken.

A heart that trusts Al-Aziz fears no man, no loss, no trial.

The world cannot shake the one who stands firm in His strength.

He humbles the mighty and raises the forgotten.

True strength is not in the hands, but in the heart that relies on Him.

To stand with Al-Aziz is to stand unshaken in a crumbling world.

"The upper hand is better than the lower hand (i.e., the one who gives is better than the one who receives)."
Sahih Bukhari

9. Al-Jabbar الجَبَّارُ (The Compeller)

The name "Al-Jabbār" The Compeller is mentioned once in the Qur'an.

Key Verses: *Mentioned in Surah Al-Hashr (59:23)*

The world will break you. The weight of sorrow will bend your spine, and despair will press upon your chest like a mountain.

But listen; **Al-Jabbar** *is the Mender of the broken, the Healer of wounds unseen.*

Like a potter shaping clay, He restores what was shattered, makes whole what was lost.

Trust in His wisdom, for He compels only towards what is best.

When you cannot mend yourself, He will mend you.

Every shattered soul will be made whole in His hands.

You flee from Him, yet He gently brings you back.

You may break a thousand times, but Al-Jabbar never tires of repairing you.

His will is the wind that bends the trees, yet He is gentle with those who submit.

Do not resist what He decrees, for His guidance leads to what is best.

The one who bows to Al-Jabbar stands unbroken, no force can shake their resolve.

But those who defy must learn from the people of Ād; builders of towering pride,

Who scorned their prophet and cast the truth aside.

Then came the screaming wind, relentless and fierce,

Seven nights of wrath that brought them to their knees.

(Surah Al-Haqqah, 69:6–8)

"The most beloved deeds to Allah are those done regularly, even if they are small."
Sahih Bukhari

10. Al-Mutakabbir المُتَكَبِّرُ (The Supreme)

The name "Al-Mutakabbir" The Supreme" or "The One Supreme in Greatness is mentioned once in the Qur'an.

Key Verses: *Mentioned in Surah Al-Hashr (59:23)*

His greatness is beyond measure, yet He listen to the cries of His servants.

To Him belongs all pride, yet He calls upon us with love.

Our Lord says through his beloved messenger: "Pride (الكبرياء) is My cloak and Majesty (العظمة) is My robe. Whoever competes with Me in either of them, I will cast him into the Hellfire." Sahih Muslim

He is above all, yet He lifts up those who lower themselves before Him.

The proud are small in His sight, but the humble are made great.

The more you recognize His greatness, the more you understand your own smallness.

Do not chase status, for true elevation is in nearness to Him.

The one who stands before Al-Mutakabbir in humble surrender walks the earth with grace and dignity.

Do not resist what He decrees, for His guidance leads to what is truly best.

But let the defiant take heed from the tale of Thamūd;

They carved their homes into the hills, yet denied the truth, despite the signs.

A Camel sent by heaven's will,

But in their pride, they killed it; and all fell still.

In stone and sand, their fate is cast,

A warning echo from the past.

(Surah Ash-Shams, 91:11–15)

11. Al-Khaliq الخَالِقُ (The Creator)

The name "Al-Khāliq" The Creator is mentioned 8 times in the Qur'an

Key Verses: *Mentioned in 6:102, 13:16, 39:62*

*Have you ever tried to count the stars? To trace the pattern of a butterfly's wing? To hold time in your hand? You cannot. For it is **Al-Khaliq**; The Creator; who brings forth wonders from the void, shaping existence with a command:*

Be! And it is. *(Quran 36:82)*

No artist, no scientist, no dreamer can match His creation.

"He is Allah, the Creator, the Maker, the Fashioner." *(Quran 59:24)*

Before time began, before the first breath of the universe, He willed all into being.

Every atom, every heartbeat, every star in the sky is a verse in His endless creation.

You were formed in the unseen, designed with precision beyond your knowing.

To witness Al-Khaliq, look at the patterns of the stars of the galaxies.

Some stars you see tonight... died a thousand years ago.

Yet their light just reached your eyes; a delayed celestial glow.

That's how vast the universe is, stretching far beyond your sight,

And yet you think you grasp it all in your fleeting, borrowed light?

You are but a speck in this infinite span,

A breath, a blink, a vapor; part of a greater plan.

So, bow not to ego, nor science alone,

But to the One who placed each star upon its throne.

The cosmos obeys Him, galaxies revolve by His will,

Every atom, every pulse; perfectly still... until He commands.

He is the Creator; timeless, supreme, divine,

And everything you see... is only a sign.

"Initially, there was nothing but Allah, and then He created His Throne. His throne was over the water, and He wrote everything in the Book (in Heaven) and created the Heavens and the Earth."
Sahih al-Bukhari (Hadith 3191

12. Al-Bari البَارِئ (The Evolver)

The name "Al-Bāri'" The Evolver/ The Maker is mentioned once in the Qur'an.

Key Verses: *Mentioned in 59:24*

"He is Allah, the Creator, the Inventor, the Fashioner; to Him belong the best names. Whatever is in the heavens and earth exalts Him. And He is the Exalted in Might, the Wise." *Surah Al-Hashr (59:24)*

Nothing remains as it was; He molds, He refines, He transforms.
You are not who you were yesterday, nor will you be tomorrow; He is shaping you still.
Every hardship is a chisel in the hands of Al-Bari, sculpting you into your true form.
You wish to stay the same, but He knows what you are meant to become.
Even the seed in darkness does not resist becoming a tree; why do you resist your own growth?
Do not fear change, for it is the sign of His work within you.
Surrender to His shaping, and you will emerge more beautiful than you imagined.

13. Al-Musawwir المُصَوِّرُ (The Fashioner)

The name "Al-Musawwir" The Fashioner is mentioned once in the Qur'an.

Key Verses: *Mentioned in 59:24*

"Indeed, We created man in the best form (or stature)."

Surah At-Tin 95:4

He did not just create you; He designed you with love, down to the last detail.

Your voice, your eyes, the lines on your hands; each is a signature of Al-Musawwir.

No two faces, no two souls, are alike; every being is a unique masterpiece.

Even your imperfections are part of His divine artistry; do not despise what He has formed.

He who shaped the petals of the rose and the wings of the bird has shaped your destiny, too.

If He crafted you with care, why do you compare yourself to others?

Honor the shape He has given you, for He makes no mistakes in His design.

The Prophet Muhammad told us:

"The human being has 360 joints. Whoever honors them by giving charity for each joint; through an act of good or removing harm or guiding others; will walk that day away from Hell."

Sahih Muslim (1007)

14. Al-Ghaffar الغَفَّارُ (The Constant Forgiver)

The name "Al-Ghaffār" The Constant Forgiver is mentioned 5 times in the Qur'an.

Key Verses: *Mentioned in 20:82, 38:66, 39:5*

---

*No sin is too great for His forgiveness. He is **Al-Ghaffar**, the One who forgives repeatedly, and **Al-Afuww**, the One who erases sins as if they never existed.*

"Say, 'O My servants who have transgressed against themselves [by sinning], do not despair of the mercy of Allah. Indeed, Allah forgives all sins.'" *(Quran 39:53)*

No matter how far you have strayed, His door is always open.

Your sins rise like waves, but His forgiveness is an endless ocean.
No matter how many times you fall, He waits for you to return.
You tire of seeking forgiveness, but He never tires of granting it.
The world may define you by your past, but Al-

Ghaffar sees only your return.
The stain of sin is heavy, but a single sincere tear washes it away.
Turn back, even if a thousand times; you will find His door always open.
To be forgiven is to be born anew; walk forward in the light of His mercy.

"No one forgives except that Allah increases him in honor."
Sahih Muslim

15. Al-Qahhar القَهَّارُ (The All-Prevailing One)

The name "Al-Qahhār" The All-Prevailing One is mentioned 6 times in the Qur'an.

Key Verses: *Mentioned in 12:39, 14:48, 39:4*

"And He is the Supreme (prevailing) over His servants." Surah Al-An'am 6:18

None stand against Him, yet He is gentle to those who submit.
Better to surrender and trust to your Lord.
He is the force behind the rising sun and the falling tyrant.
Every hardship is His way of breaking what is false within you.
To resist Him is to struggle in vain; to yield is to find peace.
The heart that bows to Al-Qahhar stands unshaken before all else.

"The strong is not the one who overcomes the people by his strength, but the strong is the one who controls himself while in anger."
Sahih Bukhari

16. Al-Wahhab الوَهَّابُ (The Supreme Bestower)

The name "Al-Wahhāb" The Supreme Bestower is mentioned 3 times in the Qur'an.

Key Verses: *Mentioned in 3:8, 38:9, 38:35*

The sun does not ask for gratitude as it bathes the world in gold. The rain does not demand payment as it quenches the thirst of the land. Al-Wahhab, the Bestower; He gives without condition, without expectation.

"Or do they have treasures of the mercy of your Lord, the Exalted in Might, the Bestower?" *(Quran 38:9)*

The greatest gifts are not counted in wealth or measured in status.

They are peace in the heart, love in the soul, and the ability to see beauty even in pain. And He, Al-Wahhab, grants these freely to those who open their hands to receive.

What is yours was never yours; it was always a gift from Al-Wahhab.

He gives without measure, without expectation, without limit.
You do not need to earn His gifts; He bestows them out of mercy.
Every breath, every moment, every blessing is from Him; have you thanked Him today?
The more you seek, the more He bestows upon you.
To seek from Al-Wahhab is never to seek in vain.
Ask, and you will receive; not always what you want, but always what you need.

"And your Lord says, 'Call upon Me; I will respond to you.'" Surah Ghafir 40:60

Encourage those around you to reflect on this wisdom and embody its meaning in their lives. Let it inspire kindness and deeper understanding in their hearts.

"The most beloved of people to Allah are those who are most beneficial to people."
Sahih Muslim

17. Ar-Razzaq الرَّزَّاقُ (The Provider)

---

*The name "**Ar-Razzaq**" The Provider is mentioned 1 time in the Qur'an*

Key Verses: *Mentioned in 51:58*

Walk in the wilderness and observe: the ant scurrying with its provision, the bird that sings as dawn breaks, knowing its sustenance is already written.

Not a soul moves, not a breath is taken, but that it is sustained by Ar-Razzaq, The Provider.

He provides for the believer and the disbeliever, for the grateful and the heedless.

He feeds the fish in the darkest depths of the ocean and the child nestled in its mother's embrace.

"Allah is the Provider, the Possessor of Strength, the Firm." *(Quran 51:58)*

O traveler of this world, why do you fear? Your provision was written before you took your first breath. Strive, but do not despair.

Work, but do not forget: the One who provides is the One who loves you more than you can fathom.

The bird leaves its nest with an empty stomach but returns with food; so too will He provide for you.

What is written for you will reach you, even if all the world tries to withhold it.
The wealth of kings is dust before the abundance of Ar-Razzaq.
He who feeds the whale in the deep sea and the deer in the quiet forest will not forget you.
Do not chase provision; chase Him, and provision will chase you.
Your sustenance is in His hands, not in your fears.
A heart that trusts Ar-Razzaq will never know the hunger of anxiety.

And always remember your prophet teaching

"Do not envy one another, do not hate one another, do not turn away from one another, and be servants of Allah as brothers."

Sahih Muslim

18. Al-Fattah الفَتَّاحُ (The Supreme Solver)

The name "Al-Fattāḥ" The Supreme Solver (The Opener, The Judge) is mentioned once in the Qur'an.

Key Verses: *Mentioned in 34:26*

Remember when Prophet Musa (Moses) and his people were trapped between Pharaoh's army and the Red Sea, he cried:

"Indeed, with me is my Lord; He will guide me." *(Surah Ash-Shu'ara, 26:62).*
Allah responded by **opening** *the sea, creating a path to salvation*

Every locked door has a key, and He holds them all.
Where you see walls, He creates pathways.
You knock in desperation, but He has already opened another door.
Do not despair at closed opportunities; He closes only to lead you to something greater.
He removes obstacles as easily as the dawn removes the night.
Even when you do not understand, trust that He is unlocking what is best for you.
To call upon Al-Fattah is to invite solutions you never imagined.

We all remember this story from

Sahih al-Bukhari (No. 5974)

about the three men sought shelter in a cave,
Then a boulder blocked their way.
With no escape, they turned above,
And called on Allah, each with a sincere deed of love:

The first stood all night with milk in hand,
Refusing to drink until his parents could stand.

The second gave up a forbidden desire,
Out of fear of Allah, though his heart was on fire.

The third returned wealth to a man long gone,
Investing his wage until he came back drawn.

They asked: "O Allah! If we did this for You alone…
Relieve us from this stone!"
The rock moved with every plea,
Until at last, they walked out free.

19. Al-'Alim العَلِيمُ (The All-Knowing)

The name "Al-'Alīm" The All-Knowing is mentioned 157 times in the Qur'an.

Key Verses: *Mentioned in 2:32, 3:92, 4:35, 6:73*

"And He knows what you earn (or acquire or commit)." *Surah Al-An'am (6:3)*

He knows the secret sorrows you hide, the prayers you whisper in the night.
Before you speak, before you even think, He knows what is in your heart.
He sees beyond what you show the world; nothing is hidden from Al-'Alim.
You plan, you worry, you doubt; but He already knows what is best for you.
If you knew what He knows, you would trust Him completely.
His wisdom is woven into every moment of your life; watch for the signs.
Seek knowledge, but remember: True wisdom is knowing that He knows best.

The Prophet said, **"The best among you (Muslims) are those who learn the Qur'an and teach it."**

Sahih al-Bukhari (Hadith 5027)

20. Al-Qabid القَابِضُ (The Withholder)

The name "Al-Qābid" The Withholder does not explicitly appear in the Qur'an in this exact form. However, the concept of Allah withholding and constricting is mentioned in various verses using related words.

Key Verses: Mentioned in 2:245

Remember the Prophet taught us

"If you ask, ask Allah; if you seek help, seek it from Allah. And know that if the whole nation were to gather to benefit you with something, they would not benefit you except with what Allah has already written for you. And if they gathered to harm you, they would not harm you except with what Allah has written against you."

What you beg for may be what He withholds; for He sees what you cannot.
The drought teaches gratitude for the rain.
Do not despair when your hands are empty; He withholds only to give at the right time.
Sometimes the absence of a thing is the greatest gift of all.
He holds back not to punish, but to protect.
What is kept from you today may be preparing you

*for something greater tomorrow.
Trust in His wisdom, even when your prayers seem unanswered.*

Take a second and look around, you're already living something you once prayed for.

Allah withholding is actually a giving

21. Al-Basit البَاسِط (The Extender)

The name "Al-Bāsit" The Extender does not explicitly appear in the Qur'an in this exact form. However, the concept of Allah extending or granting abundance is mentioned in several verses using related words.

Key Verses: *Mentioned in 2:245*

"Allah extends provision for whom He wills and restricts it. And they rejoice in the worldly life, while the worldly life is not, compared to the Hereafter, except a (brief) enjoyment." *Surah Ar-Ra'd (13:26)*

When He extends His hand of generosity, no one can limit what He gives.
A soul suffocated by despair will find breath again when Al-Basit expands its chest.
The horizon stretches beyond what your eyes can see; so too does His mercy.
When you feel confined by the world, know that He can make space for you.
Your heart feels heavy, your path feels narrow; but wait, for Al-Basit will widen both.
Do not cling to what limits you; open your hands, and He will fill them.

When He expands your provisions, expand your gratitude.

Be thankful to your Lord in the sunshine of joy and the storm of sorrow alike,

let gratitude be the candle that lights the way, even when the path is obscured.

And don't forget to reflect that around you

"Whoever does not thank people has not thanked Allah."
Sahih Bukhari

22. Al-Khafid الخَافِضُ (The Reducer)

The name Al-Khafid (The Reducer) is not explicitly mentioned in the Qur'an. However, it is commonly recognized as one of the 99 names of Allah in Islamic tradition. Some scholars, such as Ibn Uthaymeen, Ibn Hazm, and Ibn Hajar, have excluded it from their lists due to differing criteria for what qualifies as a name of Allah.

Key Verses: Mentioned in 56:3

Observe how our Lord portrays the Day of Judgment:

"(It will) bring down (some) and raise up (others)."

Surah Al-Waqi'ah (56:3)

On that day, the unrighteous will be humbled, while the virtuous will be elevated.

He lowers the proud and brings arrogance to its knees.
When the heart grows too full of itself, He humbles it to make space for Him.
You build your towers of pride, but Al-Khafid can bring them down in an instant.

The false mighty fall because they forget Who is truly the Great.

The false mighty stumble and fall, forgetting Who reigns above all.

Let us not forget this truth:

In lands of old where tyrants stood,

Pharaoh declared with prideful breath,

'O chiefs, no god exists for you but myself!'

(Surah Al-Qasas, 28:38)

Yet their homes now lie in silence, lost for good,

And you dwell upon their shadows, where their echoes once stood.

Signs of their fate are clear as day;

Take heed, and bow humbly without delay.

For sometimes He lowers to lift you high,

Guiding with wisdom none can defy.

When He humbles, do not resist; He may shield you from harm unseen.

Better to bow in willing grace than face the force of humbled disgrace.

"He who humbles himself for Allah, Allah will raise him."
Sahih Muslim

23. Ar-Rafi الرَّافِعُ (The Exalter)

The name Ar-Rafi (The Exalter) is not explicitly mentioned verbatim in the Quran as one of the 99 Names, but it is derived from Allah's actions and attributes described in the Quran and Hadith.

Key Verses: *Mentioned in 6:83*

"**Allah will raise those who have believed among you and those who were given knowledge, by degrees. And Allah is Acquainted with what you do.**" *Surah Al-Mujadilah (58:11)*

You may be hidden today, but Al-Rafi sees you and will elevate you in His perfect time.
Do not seek status in the eyes of people; seek to be raised by Him.
A heart bowed in sincerity is worth more to Him than a throne raised in arrogance.
He exalts those who humble themselves, for humility is the ladder to the divine.
No rank, no power, no wealth can surpass the honor given by Al-Rafi.
Seek nearness to Him, and He will lift you to heights beyond this world.

24. Al-Mu'izz الْمُعِزُّ (The Honourer-Bestower)

The name "Al-Mu'izz" is not explicitly mentioned verbatim in the Quran as one of the 99 Names, but it is derived from Allah's actions and attributes described in the Quran and Hadith.

Key Verses: *Mentioned in 3:26, 28:5*

"You honor whom You will and You humble whom You will." *Surah Al-Imran (3:26)*

Honor is not in titles, wealth, or status; it is in His hands alone.

If He honors you, no one can take it away; if He withholds, no one can grant it.

The world may overlook you, but if Al-Mu'izz honors you, you have all that you need.

The truly honored are those who seek His pleasure above all else.

Do not chase the recognition of people; chase the honor of being loved by Him.

A Journey from Collapse to Clarity   *Dr. Ashi Ezz*

*He lifts the unknown into greatness when their hearts are pure.
A crown placed by Al-Mu'izz can never be removed.*

Let that wisdom guide your daily actions, shaping how you engage with the world around you.

"He who does not show mercy to our young ones and does not acknowledge the rights of our elders is not one of us."
Sahih Bukhari

25. Al-Mudhill المُذِلُّ (The Dishonourer)

The name "Al-Mudhīl" is not explicitly mentioned verbatim in the Quran as one of the 99 Names, but it is derived from Allah's actions and attributes described in the Quran and Hadith.

Key Verses: *Mentioned in 3:26, 6:93*

"And he whom Allah humiliates; for him there is no bestower of honor. Indeed, Allah does what He wills." Surah Al-Hajj (22:18)

The one who walks in arrogance will stumble, for He brings down the proud.
Dishonor is not in poverty or loss; it is in the absence of His light.
If He lowers you, it is not to harm you, but to wake you from illusions.
Power built on falsehood crumbles before the truth of Al-Mudhill.
The mightiest rulers fall when they forget Who truly rules.
Do not seek to humiliate others, for He alone decides who rises and who falls.
True dishonor is not in worldly shame but in turning away from Him.

Learn from your prophet and act with wisdom; be a beacon of light for others, not a shadow that dims their spirit.

"The believer does not curse others, is not vulgar, and is not shameless."
Sahih Muslim

26. As-Sami اَلسَّمِيعُ (The All-Hearing)

The name "As-Samī" The All-Hearing is mentioned 46 times in the Qur'an.

Key Verses: *Mentioned in 2:137, 8:24*

Listen to this

"Have you not considered that Allah knows whatever is in the heavens and whatever is on the earth? There is no private conversation of three but that He is the fourth of them, nor of five but that He is the sixth of them, nor of less than that nor more, except that He is with them wherever they are. Then, on the Day of Resurrection, He will inform them of what they did. Indeed, Allah is Knowing of all things."

(Surah Al-Mujadila 58:7)

He hears the whispers of your heart before you find the words to speak them.
No cry is unheard, no prayer is lost; Al-Sami listens to all.
Even the silent plea, buried deep within, reaches Him louder than a shout.
Speak to Him, even if the world does not listen; He is always near.

He hears you in your pain, in your longing, in your hope.
You do not need perfect words; you only need sincerity.
In the quiet of the night, in the noise of the day; He hears you and always avoid hypocrite actions.

"The signs of a hypocrite are three: when he speaks, he lies; when he makes a promise, he breaks it; and when he is entrusted, he betrays the trust."
Sahih Bukhari

27. Al-Basir البَصِيرُ (The All-Seeing)

The name "Al-Baṣīr" The All-Seeing is mentioned 42 times in the Qur'an.

Key Verses: *Mentioned in 2:110, 3:15*

"Indeed, Allah knows the unseen of the heavens and the earth. And Allah is All-Seeing of what you do." *Surah Al-Hujurat (49:18)*

He sees the tear before it falls, the wound before it bleeds, the longing before it is spoken.
The deeds done in darkness are not hidden from Him.
Even the smallest act of kindness does not go unnoticed.
You see the surface, but Al-Basir sees the depth of all things.
What you think is unseen, He has already recorded.
Do not fear being misunderstood by the world; He sees you as you truly are.
Live as if He is watching, because He always is.

"The honest and trustworthy merchant will be with the Prophets, the truthful, and the martyrs."
Sahih Bukhari

28. Al-Hakam الحَكَمُ (The Impartial Judge)

The name "Al-Ḥakam" The Impartial Judge is mentioned one time in the Qur'an.

Key Verses: Mentioned in 6:114

"Then is it other than Allah I should seek as judge while it is He who has revealed to you the Book [i.e., the Quran] explained in detail?"

Surah Al-An'am (6:114)

The world is full of false judgments, but His is the only one that matters.

Do not rush to judge others; leave it to Al-Hakam, who sees all.

His justice is not bound by time; what is unfair now will be made right.

People may misunderstand you, but He knows the truth of every heart.

Trust His judgment, even when you do not understand it.

He weighs every action, every word, with perfect balance.

When the world is unjust, remember: His verdict is final.

Even for non-Muslims, our Lord commands justice:
'And do not be an advocate for those who betray trust.'
(Qur'an, Surah An-Nisa, 4:105)

Scholars recount the tale behind this verse:
A man stole and blamed a Jew,
He cloaked the truth, as liars do.
The Prophet leaned toward what seemed fair,
But God's revelation laid truth bare.

From Heaven descended guidance clear:
'Do not side with those who deceive and smear.'
Though lies roared loud, the truth prevailed,
Al-Hakam rules where all else has failed.

29. Al-'Adl العَدْل (The Just One)

The name "Al-'Adl" The Just One is not directly mentioned in the Qur'an by this exact name. However, the concept of justice is mentioned frequently throughout the Qur'an, often using words such as "al-'adl" or describing Allah's justice.

Key Verses: Mentioned in 4:40, 3:182

"Indeed, Allah does not wrong (even) the weight of an atom; and if there is a good deed, He multiplies it and gives from Himself a great reward." *(Surah An-Nisa 4:40)*

Injustice may reign for a moment, but Al-'Adl reigns for eternity.

He rights every wrong, even if it takes lifetimes to see.

If He delays justice, it is not neglect; it is wisdom. The oppressed have no need for revenge, for Al-'Adl will bring perfect balance.

Trust in His fairness, even when the world seems cruel.

He does not forget, He does not overlook; His justice is absolute.

What is taken from you unjustly will be restored by Him in ways you cannot imagine.

The Prophet taught us that establishing justice among people is a Sadaqa (charitable gift)

Sahih al-Bukhari Hadith 2706

30. Al-Latif اللَّطِيفُ (The Subtle One)

The name "Al-Laṭīf" The Subtle One is mentioned 7 times in the Qur'an.

Key Verses: *Mentioned in 29:69, 42:19, 67:14*

His presence is like the wind, you do not see it, but you feel its touch.

"And for Allah is the highest example. And He is the Almighty, the All-Wise."

Surah An-Nahl (16:60)

The smallest blessings and the quietest mercies are His whispers of grace.

You search for grand signs but forget to look within, at the hidden blessings.

Consider your heart, your kidneys, your liver, even the good bacteria in your stomach, all silently working for you.

A delayed journey, a missed opportunity, an unexpected kindness; each is His subtle hand at work.

He guides you softly, through moments you barely notice.

When you think He is absent, look closer; Al-Latif is

A Journey from Collapse to Clarity *Dr. Ashi Ezz*

always near.
The greatest miracles are not always loud; they are often the softest.

"Allah is gentle and loves gentleness in all matters."
Sahih Muslim

31. Al-Khabir الخَبِيرُ (The All-Aware)

The name "Al-Khabīr" The All-Aware is mentioned 48 times in the Qur'an.

Key Verses: *Mentioned in 2:224, 5:97*

"Would He not know what He created? For He is the Subtle, the All-Aware."

Surah Al-Mulk (67:14)

He knows what is hidden beneath your words, the truths you do not speak.

You may deceive the world, but you cannot deceive Al-Khabir.

Every thought, every feeling, every secret of your soul; He is already aware.

You do not need to explain yourself to Him; He understands before you begin.

When you are lost in confusion, trust that Al-Khabir knows the way.

Do not seek validation from those who do not understand you; He knows you best.

His awareness is not distant; it is intimate, closer than your own knowing.

"Actions are judged by intentions, and everyone will be rewarded according to what they intended."
Sahih Bukhari

32. Al-Halim الحَلِيمُ (The Most Forbearing)

The name "Al-Ḥalīm" The Most Forbearing is mentioned 15 times in the Qur'an.

Key Verses: Mentioned in 3:155, 7:199

He sees our sins, yet does not punish us immediately. He watches our mistakes, yet gives us time to repent.

He is **Al-Haleem**, the One who is patient with His creation, waiting for them to return.

"And if Allah were to punish people for their wrongdoing, He would not leave on the earth a single creature."

(Quran 16:61)

He does not rush to punish, though He sees all. His patience with you is greater than your patience with yourself.

If He gave each their due instantly, none would stand; but Al-Halim waits, hoping for return.

A single step toward Him is met with oceans of mercy.

You stumble, yet He holds back His justice, giving you time to rise again.

His gentleness is not weakness, but the perfection of mercy.

If He is patient with you, be patient with others.

"Every act of kindness is charity."
Sahih Muslim

33. Al-'Azim العَظيمُ (The Magnificent)

The name "Al-'Azīm" The Magnificent is mentioned more than 8 times in the Qur'an.

Key Verses: Mentioned in 3:18, 62:1

"...His Throne extends over the heavens and earth, and their preservation tires Him not. And He is the Most High, the Magnificent."

Surah Al-Baqarah (2:255)

His greatness is beyond words, beyond thought, beyond imagination.
The universe is vast, yet it is but a shadow of His majesty.
Mountains crumble, empires fall, but He remains, unchanged, unshaken.
To understand His greatness, look within; your heart beats by His will.
He is beyond need, yet He tends to the smallest of creatures with care.
His magnificence is not only in power, but in the love with which He rules.
The one who knows Al-'Azim walks with humility, for all else is small before Him.

"The best deed is faith in Allah and His Messenger..." *(Bukhari 26)*

34. Al-Ghaffur الغَفُورُ (The Great Forgiver)

The name "Al-Ghaffūr" The Great Forgiver is mentioned more than 90 times in the Qur'an.

Key Verses: *Mentioned in 3:135, 4:110*

"Say, 'O My servants who have transgressed against themselves [by sinning], do not despair of the mercy of Allah. Indeed, Allah forgives all sins. Indeed, it is He who is the Forgiving, the Merciful.'"

Surah Az-Zumar (39:53)

If your sins stretched as vast as the ocean's span, His forgiveness would still be greater, beyond what man can imagine.

The door to return is never shut, no matter how far you've wandered or what you've done.

He forgives, not reluctantly, but as an eternal act of His divine nature.

Each mistake is a chance to know Him, to discover the mercy of Al-Ghaffur.

True peace is not found in being flawless, but in trusting that Al-Ghaffur always welcomes you back with open arms.

Sahih al-Bukhari, Hadith No. 4072 reminds us of Hind, who burned with rage and sought revenge.

She sent Wahshi with a spear so swift, to Uhud's field to kill Hamzah, the Prophet's cherished uncle.

Yet even then, forgiveness triumphed strong.

Time passed, and Makkah bowed to divine light;

Hind embraced Islam's truth and grace, her fiery heart transformed.

Wahshi, too, sought faith anew; even a soul once fed by hatred can be healed when truth shines through.

Forgive like the Prophet, with calm and justice,

For every soul carries sacred dust, and mercy lifts us all.

35. Ash-Shakur الشَّكُورُ (The Most Appreciative)

The name "Ash-Shakūr" The Most Appreciative appears four times in the Qur'an.

Key Verses: Mentioned in 35:30, 35:34, 42:23

---

*"**If you lend Allah a goodly loan, He will multiply it for you and forgive you. For Allah is Most Appreciative, Most Forbearing**."*

Surah At-Taghābun (64:17)

He sees the smallest of deeds and multiplies them beyond measure.

A single drop of sincerity is met with oceans of reward.

He does not need your worship, yet He appreciates it more than you can imagine.

Even a single grateful breath is written for you as an act of worship.

Give a little, and He returns it a thousandfold.

He is not in need of you, yet He cherishes every effort you make for his sake.

The heart that knows Ash-Shakur finds joy in every moment of gratitude.

"Do you know what backbiting is? It is to mention about your brother what he dislikes..." *(Bukhari 6045)*

36. Al-'Aliyy العَلِيّ (The Most High, The Exalted)

The exact name "Al-'Aliyy" The Most High, The Exalted appears eight times in the Qur'an.

Key Verses: Mentioned in 2:255, 4:34, 22:62

"That is because Allah is the Truth, and what they call upon besides Him is falsehood, and because Allah is the Most High, the Grand."

Surah Luqmān (31:30)

Above all thrones, above all heavens, above all that exists; He alone is truly High.

He is beyond reach, yet closer than your own soul.

His greatness does not distance Him; rather, it draws the sincere nearer.

Raise your hands in prayer, and know you call upon the Most High.

No power, no ruler, no force can compare to Him.

If you wish to rise, lower yourself before Al-'Aliyy.

His elevation is not one of distance, but of unmatched perfection.

"Every deed of the son of Adam is multiplied; a good deed by ten times its value, up to 700 times..."

(Bukhari 1904)

37. Al-Kabir الكَبِيرُ (The Most Great)

The name "Al-Kabīr" The Most Great appears more than 3 times in the Qur'an.

Key Verses: *Mentioned in 13:9, 22:62, 31:30*

"Knower of the unseen and the witnessed, the All-Great, the Exalted."

Surah Ar-Ra'd (13:9)

The universe is vast, yet it is but a speck before Al-Kabir.

Every greatness in creation is but a reflection of His greatness.

The greatest knowledge is to know how small we are before Him.

Nothing is beyond Him, and nothing is too small for His care.

He does not require recognition, yet the stars, the oceans, and the winds praise Him.

The one who knows Al-Kabir walks humbly, for all greatness belongs to Him.

Power in this world is fleeting, but His greatness is eternal.

"If Allah wants to do good to someone, He gives him understanding of the religion."

(Bukhari 71)

38. Al-Hafiz الحَفِيظُ (The Preserver)

The name "Al-Hafiz" The Preserver appears in the Qur'an in 12 times.

Key Verses: *Mentioned in 11:57, 34:21, 42:6*

Who watches over you when you sleep? Who shields you from the blows you never saw coming? Who lifts the forgotten and humbles the arrogant?

It is **Al-Hafiz**, the Guardian, who protects with a love greater than a mother's embrace.

"**Allah is your Protector, and He is the best of helpers**." (Quran 3:150)

He guards your heart when you are unaware of its fragility.

What is meant for you will reach you, for Al-Hafiz protects all that is yours.

The earth spins, the stars move, yet He holds everything in perfect balance.

Your breath, your steps, your unseen struggles; He preserves them all.

Nothing is lost when it is entrusted to Al-Hafiz.

He guards the sincere from harm and preserves their goodness for eternity.

The one who places their trust in Al-Hafiz walks without fear.

"Look at those below you (in worldly matters) and not at those above you, so you will not undervalue Allah's blessings."

(Bukhari 6490)

39. Al-Muqit المُقيت (The Sustainer)

The name "Al-Muqīt" The Sustainer appears once in the Qur'an.

Key Verses: *Mentioned in 4:85*

"Whoever intercedes for a good cause will have a share in its reward, and whoever intercedes for an evil cause will bear a share of its burden. And Allah is the Sustainer of all things."

Surah An-Nisā (4:85)

Every morsel you eat, every breath you take, is by His provision.

He sustains not just the body, but the soul longing for meaning.

The worms move in the dark under the dust, yet He feeds them daily.

Do not fear lack; Al-Muqit has already written your sustenance.

He nourishes hearts with guidance as He nourishes the earth with rain.

Your needs are known to Him before you even feel them.

Those who trust in Al-Muqit never go hungry; in body or in spirit.

"Whoever says in the morning and evening, 'SubhanAllah wa bihamdihi' 100 times, no one will come on the Day of Resurrection with anything better..."

(Bukhari 6406)

40. Al-Hasib الحَسِيبُ (The Reckoner)

The name "Al-Hasib" The Reckoner appears 4 times in the Qur'an.

Key Verses: *Mentioned in 4:6, 4:86, 33:39*

"Indeed, Allah is ever, over all things, an Accountant." *Surah An-Nisa (4:86)*

Every deed, every word, every intention is recorded; nothing is forgotten.

He does not overlook an atom's weight of good or evil.

His justice is perfect, balancing the scales of all existence.

Do not despair in wrongdoing, nor be arrogant in goodness; He counts all things fairly.

He is the one who settles accounts with perfect wisdom.

The world may forget your struggles, but Al-Hasib has written them all.

If you wish for ease in the reckoning, live as if He is watching; because He is.

Abu Huraira reported that the Messenger of Allah said: ***He who purifies himself in his house and then walks to one of the houses of Allah (mosques) in order to fulfil one of the obligatory duties enjoined by Allah, one step of his will wipe out his sins and the other will elevate his rank.***

Muslim Hadith 1555

41. Al-Jalil الجَلِيل (The Majestic)

The exact name "Al-Jalīl" The Majestic does not appear in the Qur'an. However, the attribute of majesty is conveyed through the phrase "Dhū al-Jalāl wa al-Ikrām" Possessor of Majesty and Honor, which appears twice in the Qur'an

Key Verses: *Mentioned in 55:27, 55:78*

"But the Face of your Lord, full of Majesty and Honor, will remain forever."

Surah Ar-Rahman (55:27)

His presence commands awe, yet His mercy invites closeness.

To recognize His majesty is to surrender in humility.

All beauty, all grandeur, all power in this world is but a reflection of Al-Jalil.

Mountains bow, seas tremble, and the heavens are held by His command.

The one who sees Al-Jalil in all things walks with reverence.

Majesty is not in outward strength but in the power of truth.

To know His majesty is to see beyond the illusion of worldly greatness.

"A man's prayer in congregation is 27 times more rewarding than his prayer alone."

(Bukhari 645)

42. Al-Karim الكَرِيمُ (The Most Generous, The Most Esteemed)

The name "Al-Karīm" The Most Generous, The Most Esteemed appears three times in the Qur'an.

Key Verses: *Mentioned in 27:40, 82:6*

"O mankind, what has deceived you concerning your Lord, the Most Generous?"
Surah Al-Infitar (82:6)

He gives without measure, without condition, without limit.
You ask for a drop, and He grants oceans.
His generosity does not diminish; each gift is a sign of infinite bounty.
The hands that give are beloved to Al-Karim.
If you wish to receive, begin by giving.
The wealth of this world fades, but the generosity of Al-Karim never ends.
To know Al-Karim is to trust that you will never be left empty-handed.

*"**Eat, drink, give charity, and wear clothes as long as it does not involve extravagance or pride**."*

(Bukhari 5635)

43. Ar-Raqib الرَّقِيبُ (The Watchful)

---

name "Ar-Raqīb" The Watchful appears four times in the Qur'an.

Key Verses: Mentioned in 4:1, 5:117

"And ever is Allah, over all things, an Observer." Surah Al-Ahzab (33:52)

No action is too small, no thought too hidden; He sees all.
With eyes of punishment, or with eyes of love and guidance, it is your choice.
When you are alone, He is there. When you are lost, He is near.
The world forgets, but Ar-Raqib remembers.
Live not in fear of His watchfulness, but in awe of His care.
When you feel unseen, remember Ar-Raqib has never taken His gaze off you.
To walk with awareness of Ar-Raqib is to walk in truth.

"When you go to bed, recite Ayat al-Kursi, for there will remain over you a guardian from Allah..."

(Bukhari 2311)

44. Al-Mujib المُجِيبُ (The Responsive One)

The exact name "Al-Mujīb" The Responsive One appears once in the Qur'an.

Key Verses: *Mentioned in 11:61*

"And when My servants ask you concerning Me, indeed I am near. I respond to the supplicant when he calls upon Me. So let them respond to Me and believe in Me that they may be guided."

Surah Al-Baqarah (2:186)

Every whispered prayer reaches Him.
He does not delay, nor does He ignore; He responds in the perfect way, at the perfect time.
Sometimes the answer is immediate, sometimes it is hidden in patience, sometimes it is beyond what you imagined.
He hears the silent prayers of your heart before they are formed into words.
If you do not hear His response, perhaps you are listening for the wrong answer.
To trust Al-Mujib is to know that every call is met with divine wisdom.

"Avoid the seven destructive sins..." including slandering chaste women. *(Bukhari 2766)*

45. Al-Wasi' الوَاسِعُ (The All-Encompassing, The Boundless)

The name "Al-Wāsi'" The All-Encompassing, The Boundless is mentioned nine times in the Qur'an.

Key Verses: *Mentioned in 2:268, 2:261, 2:247*

His mercy does not run dry. His generosity does not wane. The heavens and the earth, the past and the future, the known and the unknown; all are encompassed by Him, Al-Wasi, The All-Encompassing.

"Indeed, Allah is All-Encompassing, All-Knowing." *(Quran 2:115)*

No sin is too great for His forgiveness. No distance is too far for His embrace.

Dive deep into His mercy, and you will find yourself carried by its waves.

His mercy has no limits, His knowledge has no boundaries.
The sky, the earth, the universe cannot contain Him; yet He dwells within the heart that seeks Him.
No soul is too far, no sin too great; His vastness

holds space for all.
Do not define yourself by your limits when you are embraced by Al-Wasi'.
You may feel small, but you exist within the boundlessness of His presence.
He is beyond time, beyond space, beyond the grasp of thought; yet He is with you.
To know Al-Wasi' is to know that you are never lost, never outside His reach.

"Whoever believes in Allah and the Last Day, let him maintain good relations with his relatives."

(Bukhari 6138)

46. Al-Hakim الحَكِيمُ (The All-Wise)

The name "Al-Ḥakīm" The All-Wise appears in the Qur'an more than 95 times.

Key Verses: Mentioned in 2:32, 2:129, 2:260

"They said, 'Exalted are You! We have no knowledge except what You have taught us. Indeed, it is You who are the All-Knowing, the All-Wise.'" Surah Al-Baqarah (2:32)

There is no coincidence, only the wisdom of Al-Hakim unfolding.
What you call failure, He calls redirection.
What you call unanswered, He calls protection.
The wisdom of Al-Hakim is hidden in every moment, waiting to be seen.
Trusting Him is to trust that even the unanswered prayers are answered.
The one who knows Al-Hakim does not ask, "Why me?" but says, "Guide me."

"Avoid suspicion, for suspicion is the worst of false tales, and do not spy..." (Bukhari 6064)

47. Al-Wadud الوَدُودُ (The Most Loving)

The name "Al-Wadūd" The Most Loving is mentioned twice in the Qur'an.

Key Verses: *Mentioned in 11:90, 85:14*

---

*He does not just love; He is **Al-Wadud**, the source of all love. His love is eternal, unconditional, and vast beyond measure.*

"Indeed, my Lord is Merciful and Loving."
(Quran 85:14)

Seek His love, and He will place love for you in the hearts of His creation.

His love is not given in exchange; it is His essence.
He loved you before you were, and He will love you beyond time.
When the world's love is conditional, Al-Wadud remains constant.
His love is not just in ease, but in every challenge sent to refine you.
No heart that seeks Him is ever left empty.
To love for His sake is to taste the sweetness of eternity.
The one who knows Al-Wadud carries love, not just for others, but for all creation.

Learn from who

"Nor does he speak from his own desire. It is nothing but a revelation sent down [to him]."

Qur'an, Surah An-Najm (53:3–4)

"None of you truly believes until he loves for his brother what he loves for himself."

[Sahih al-Bukhari, Hadith 13; Sahih Muslim, Hadith 45]

48. Al-Majid المَجِيدُ (The Glorious, The Most Honorable)

The name "Al-Mājid" The Glorious, The Most Honorable is mentioned twice in the Qur'an.

Key Verses: *Mentioned in 85:15, 11:73*

"Or do they have the depositories of the mercy of your Lord, the All-Mighty, the Most Glorious?" *Surah Sad (38:9)*

His glory is not in display, but in the perfection of His being.

The stars shine, the sun rises, the oceans move; yet all is but a shadow of Al-Majid's splendor.

No name, no title, no status can match the majesty of Al-Majid.

The one who glorifies Him is honored in return.

He is not in need of our praise, yet He bestows honor on those who remember Him.

The one who seeks worldly recognition is soon forgotten, but the one who seeks Al-Majid is written in eternity.

To witness His glory is to bow in fear and hope, not just in love.

"Nothing is more honorable to Allah than supplication." *(Bukhari 6346)*

49. Al-Ba'ith الْبَاعِثُ (The Infuser of New Life)

The name "Al-Bā'ith" The Infuser of New Life is mentioned 3 times in the Qur'an.

Key Verses: *Mentioned in 62:9, 22:7*

"On the Day when Allah will resurrect them all and inform them of what they did. Allah has kept account of it, while they forgot it. And Allah is a Witness over all things."

Surah Al-Mujadila (58:6)

He awakens what is dormant, revives what is lost.

He calls forth life from the dead earth and light from the darkest hearts.

No soul is too lost to be revived by Al-Ba'ith.

He resurrects not just bodies, but faith, hope, and purpose.

When you feel empty, know that He can breathe life into your spirit once more.

To know Al-Ba'ith is to believe in renewal, in new beginnings, in the possibility of transformation.

His call will come for all; what will you rise to?

"You must be truthful, for truthfulness leads to righteousness, and righteousness leads to Paradise..."

(Bukhari 6094)

50. Ash-Shahid الشَّهِيدُ (The All-and-Ever Witnessing)

The name "Ash-Shahīd" The All-and-Ever Witnessing is mentioned more than 15 times in the Qur'an.

Key Verses: *Mentioned in 4:79, 5:117*

"We will show them Our signs in the horizons and within themselves until it becomes clear to them that it is the truth. But is it not sufficient concerning your Lord that He is, over all things, a Witness?"

Surah Fussilat (41:53)

You are never truly alone; He is always present.

Every tear, every sigh, every unspoken prayer is witnessed by Ash-Shahid.

He sees not just your deeds, but your intentions, your struggles, your silent battles.

Justice in this world may fail, but Ash-Shahid misses nothing.

He is witness to your pain, and He is witness to your patience.

"Four traits make someone a pure hypocrite: When he speaks, he lies; when he promises, he breaks it..."

(Bukhari 34)

51. Al-Haqq الحَقُّ (The Absolute Truth)

The name "Al-Haqq" The Absolute Truth is mentioned 10 times in the Qur'an.

Key Verses: *Mentioned in 17:81, 22:6*

Now, let us reflect on a name that is the foundation of all reality: Al-Haqq (The Truth). Allah says:

"That is because Allah is the Truth, and it is He who gives life to the dead." *(Quran 22:6)*

When you reflect on this name, you are reminded that everything in this world is temporary, but Allah is eternal.

His promises are true, His words are true, and His existence is the ultimate truth.

In a world filled with illusions and falsehoods, Al-Haqq is the anchor that keeps us grounded.

He is the One who bring justice, who fulfill His promises, and who reveal the truth on the Day of Judgment.

Truth is not in words, but in the presence of Al-Haqq. What is false will perish, but Al-Haqq remains. Seek not truth in fleeting opinions, but in the One who is eternal.
To align with Al-Haqq is to walk the straight path,

unshaken by illusions.
The heart that submits to Al-Haqq finds clarity beyond doubt.
What you seek outside already exists within; Al-Haqq is nearer than your own breath.

"Islam is built upon five: Testimony of faith, prayer, Zakat, Hajj, and fasting Ramadan." (Bukhari 8)

52. Al-Wakil الوَكِيلُ (The Trustee)

The name **"Al-Wakil" The Trustee** is mentioned **14 times** in the **Qur'an**.

Key Verses: Mentioned in 3:173, 9:51

"So turn away from them and rely upon Allah. And sufficient is Allah as a Trustee."
Surah An-Nisā' (4:81)

*Place your trust in Him, for He will never fail.
The world may deceive, but Al-Wakil never betrays.
Every burden entrusted to Him becomes light,
Every struggle finds purpose in His infinite might.*

*You plan, you strive, you struggle and pray,
But true reliance is to surrender and obey.
When the path before you is shadowed and unclear,
Trust that Al-Wakil has already made the way appear.*

*Release what you cannot control, and find peace;
Al-Wakil's care is endless, His wisdom does not cease.*

*Look to your beloved Prophet in his moment of trial,
When all seemed lost, yet his faith did not defile.
In the Cave of Thawr, as enemies closed in,
Abu Bakr grew anxious, not for himself, but for him.*

With calming words, the Prophet reassured his friend:
'Do not be sad, indeed Allah is with us.'
And thus, the storm within came to an end.

What an absolute trust

53. Al-Qawiyy القَوِيّ (The All-Strong)

*The name "Al-Qawiyy" The All-Strong is mentioned **10 times** in the Qur'an.*

Key Verses: *Mentioned in 57:25, 11:66*

"Surely your Lord is the All-Strong, the Almighty." *Surah Hud (11:66)*

His strength is not force, but power beyond measure. The storms rage, the earth trembles, yet nothing moves without Al-Qawiyy's will.
What is strength but the ability to carry others? He lifts all who turn to Him.
No enemy is greater than the one within, and Al-Qawiyy strengthens the soul that seeks Him.
His strength is in justice, in patience, in unwavering command.
Lean on Al-Qawiyy, and you will never collapse.
To be strong is not to overpower, but to stand firm in His light. As He owns it all

"On the Day We will fold up the sky like the folding of a scroll for books. Just as We began the first creation, We will repeat it. [That is] a promise binding upon Us. Indeed, We will do it."
Qur'an, Surah Al-Anbiya (21:104)

54. Al-Matin المَتِينُ (The Firm One)

The name **"Al-Matīn"** *The Firm One* is mentioned **1 time** in the Qur'an.

Key Verses: Mentioned in 51:58

"Surely Allah is the All-Provider, the Lord of Power, the Firm." Surah Adh-Dhāriyāt (51:58)

Unshaken, unwavering, beyond time; Al-Matin holds all things in place.
The winds of change may shake the world, but He remains unchanged.
He is the anchor for the hearts that drift in uncertainty.
What is firm in Him cannot be broken by the trials of life.
When the world feels unstable, seek refuge in Al-Matin.
No hardship can overpower the one who is firm in faith.
To hold onto Al-Matin is to find stillness in the midst of chaos.

"Do not consider any act of kindness insignificant, even meeting your brother with a cheerful face."

(Bukhari 6126)

55. Al-Wali الوَلِيُّ (The Protector)

*The name "Al-Walī" The Protector is mentioned **14 times** in the **Qur'an**.*

Key Verses: *Mentioned in 42:9, 58:22, 9:116*

"Or have they taken allies besides Him? But Allah; He is the Ally, and He gives life to the dead, and He is over all things competent."
Surah Ash-Shura (42:9)

He is closer than the closest, the most faithful of companions.
When the world turns away, Al-Wali remains.
No betrayal, no abandonment, only unwavering love and mercy for who submit.
Those who walk in His path find their footsteps guided.
To know Al-Wali is to never be truly alone.
He is not just a protector but our absolute guardian.
The one who makes Al-Wali their ally walks in divine companionship.

Imagine your father gives you money to buy him a gift.

It's his; yet he smiles, receiving it from you.

Not for the gift, but for the love behind it.

Now reflect...

To Allah belongs the highest of examples.

He owns your soul, your body, your breath.

Whatever you give; was already His.

Yet He calls you to recognize the truth,

to offer back what is borrowed,

so, He may bless you even more.

But you turn away...

"And they did not appraise Allah with true appraisal" *Surah Az-Zumar (39:67)*

Be grateful.

For even your gratitude; is a gift from Him.

56. Al-Hamid الحَمِيدُ (The Most Praiseworthy)

---

*The name **"Al-Ḥamīd" The Most Praiseworthy** is mentioned **17 times** in the **Qur'an**.*

Key Verses: *Mentioned in 2:195, 3:164, 4:147*

"O humanity! You are the poor in need of Allah, while Allah is the Self-Sufficient, All-Praiseworthy." *Surah Fāṭir (35:15)*

All praise belongs to Him, for all beauty and goodness flow from Him.
Even in silence, creation praises Al-Hamid; the waves, the trees, the stars.
To praise Him is not to add to His greatness, but to awaken gratitude within yourself.
He is worthy of praise not just in ease, but in every trial that refines the soul.
A heart that remembers Al-Hamid is a heart filled with light.
To see the beauty of Al-Hamid is to see Him in all things.
The tongue that praises is blessed, but the heart that praises in hardship is beloved.

He taught us the art of praise and blessed us with tongues to speak and souls to feel.

Embrace this sacred gift with gratitude, and let it guide your steps toward the radiant light, for in every word of thanks lies a path to deeper connection and purpose.

"Allah is more pleased with the repentance of His slave than a person who loses his camel in a desert and then finds it." (Bukhari 6309)

57. Al-Muhsi الْمُحْصِي (The All-Enumerating, The Counter)

*The name **"Al-Muhsī"** The All-Enumerating, The Counter is mentioned **2 times** in the **Qur'an**.*

***Key Verses**: Mentioned in 19:94, 72:28*

"Indeed, He has enumerated them and counted them a [full] counting."

Quran 19:94

Not a single breath, not a single thought, escapes His knowledge.

He counts the drops of rain, the grains of sand, the beats of every heart.

What is hidden from man is recorded by Al-Muhsi.

No deed is lost, no act of kindness unnoticed.

When you feel forgotten, remember Al-Muhsi never loses count of your struggles.

So keep in the right path
Your prayers are numbered, and each is heard.

"No fatigue, illness, worry, sorrow, harm, or distress befalls a Muslim, even if it were a prick of a thorn, but that Allah expiates some of his sins because of it." (Bukhari 5641)

58. Al-Mubdi المُبْدِئ (The Originator, The Initiator)

The name "Al-Mubdi" The Originator, The Initiator is not explicitly mentioned in the Quran, its meaning is derived from Allah's actions and attributes described in the Quran.

Key Verses: *Mentioned in 85:13*

"Indeed, it is He who is the Originator of creation." Surah Al-Buruj (85:13)

Before all things, He was. And from nothing, He called forth existence.
He speaks, and creation awakens.
Every idea, every beginning, is a reflection of Al-Mubdi.
The seeds in the earth, the stars in the sky, all are His first touch.
What He begins, none can undo.
To trust Al-Mubdi is to trust that every ending is a door to a new beginning.
He brought you into being; do not doubt that He has a purpose for you.

"And I did not create the jinn and mankind except to worship Me."

Surah Adh-Dhariyat (51:56)

59. Al-Mu'id الْمُعِيدُ (The Restorer, The Reinstater)

*The name **"Al-Mu'id" The Restorer, The Reinstater** is not explicitly mentioned in the Quran, its meaning is derived from Allah's actions and attributes described in the Quran.*

Key Verses: Mentioned in 59:24

"It is He who begins creation, then repeats it; and that is easier for Him. To Him belongs the highest example in the heavens and the earth. And He is the Exalted in Might, the Wise." Surah Ar-Rum (30:27)

What is lost is never truly gone; Al-Mu'id restores all in its time.
He brings back what was taken, renews what was broken.
No soul is beyond return, no faith beyond rekindling.
The body perishes, but Al-Mu'id will call it forth again.
Every failure is a lesson, every loss a preparation for something greater.
When you are at your lowest, remember Al-Mu'id is the One who lifts you again.

He revives hearts, restores dignity, and grants second chances without limit.

Even if you don't attain it in this temporary life, rest assured; you will receive it in the Hereafter.

Nothing is ever truly lost.

"Every intoxicant is Khamr (wine), and every intoxicant is forbidden.*" (Bukhari 5585)*

60. Al-Muhyi المُحْيِي (The Giver of Life)

*The name "Al-Muhyī" The Giver of Life is mentioned **2 time** in the Qur'an.*

Key Verses: *Mentioned in 30:50, 41:39*

Life and death are but two breaths in the hand of Allah.

He gives life where none exists, and He calls souls home when their time is written.

*To some, this is a terror. To the believer, it is a promise; **Al-Muhyi** brings forth life in ways unseen, and **Al-Mumit** welcomes the weary back to the source of all peace.*

"It is He who gives life and causes death, and to Him you will be returned." *(Quran 10:56)*

Life is not in the body, but in the soul; and He is the giver of both.
He breathes life into the lifeless, hope into the weary.
No darkness is too deep for Al-Muhyi to illuminate.
Each morning is a sign of His power to restore.
The one who seeks Him is granted a heart that is truly alive.
Do not despair, for the one who holds onto Al-Muhyi

will never be left lifeless.
To be alive in Him is to see, to feel, to love beyond this world.

"Allah does not look at your bodies or your appearances, but He looks at your hearts and your deeds."
(Bukhari 6011)

61. Al-Mumit اَلْمُمِيتُ (The Creator of Death)

The name *"Al-Mumīt" The Creator of Death* is mentioned **2 time** in the **Qur'an**.

Key Verses: Mentioned in 40:68, 7:158

"It is Allah who created death and life to test you as to which of you is best in deed." Surah Aal-e-Imran (3:156)

He is the Creator of life, and He is the Creator of death.
Death is not an end, but a transition crafted by His hand.
Al-Mumit holds the key to the beginning and the end of all things.
In His wisdom, death is not to be feared, but understood as a passage to eternal life.
Every moment is borrowed; every breath is a gift He grants, and when it ends, He takes it in His perfect timing.
The breath you hold in your chest is His to give and His to take; live it with gratitude.
In the face of death, trust in the One who is its origin, for it is His will that we live and die.

Let us recall this story from Quran

"Or [consider] the one who passed by a town which had collapsed in ruins. He said, 'How can Allah bring this back to life after its death?' Surah Al-Baqarah, verse 259 (2:259)

> He passed by ruins, silent and dead,
> "How will God raise this?" he said.
> So Allah made him sleep that day;
> A hundred years just slipped away.
>
> His food untouched, his donkey dry,
> Then life returned before his eye.
> A sign so clear, no need to guess:
> Allah gives life, and causes death.

"The son of Adam says, 'My wealth, my wealth!' But do you own anything except what you eat and consume, wear until it wears out, or give in charity?"
(Bukhari 5939)

62. Al-Hayy الحَيُّ (The Ever-Living)

*The name "Al-Ḥayy" The Ever-Living is mentioned **five times** in the Qur'an.*

***Key Verses**: Mentioned in 2:255, 40:65*

Allah is the Ever-Living, the One whose existence has no beginning and no end. His life is perfect, unchanging, and eternal. He declares:

"Allah – there is no deity except Him, the Ever-Living, the Self-Sustaining." *(Quran 2:255)*

*Every breath you take, every heartbeat, is a gift from Him. When you feel weak or overwhelmed, turn to **Al-Hayy**, the Ever-Living, the One who sustains all existence. He never forgets, never abandons, and never ceases to be.*

Before time began, He was. When time ends, He will remain.
He is life itself; untouched by decay, unaffected by endings.
Without Him, nothing would exist; through Him, all things endure.

In moments of despair, remember that the Ever-Living is always present, sustaining and guiding.

His presence is eternal, and in Him, we find the true essence of life; everlasting, unwavering, and beyond human comprehension.

"The glance is one of the poisoned arrows of Satan. Whoever lowers his gaze for Allah, He will replace it with sweetness of faith he will find in his heart."
(Bukhari 6226)

63. Al-Qayyum القَيُّومُ (The Sustainer, The Self-Subsisting)

The name *"Al-Qayyūm" The Sustainer, The Self-Subsisting* is mentioned **3 times** in the **Qur'an**.

Key Verses: Mentioned in 3:2, 20:111

Allah is the One who sustains all of creation. He is independent of everything, while everything depends on Him. He says:
"He is the Sustainer of [all] existence." (Quran 3:2)

*This name teaches us to rely on Allah completely. No matter how powerful or self-sufficient you may feel, you are ultimately dependent on Him. When you call upon **Al-Qayyum**, you are acknowledging that He is the One who manages all affairs, who provides for you, and who protects you. He is the One who holds the universe in His hands and yet still hears your whispered prayers.*

The world stands not by its own strength, but by His will.
Al-Qayyum needs no support, yet He supports all things.
Everything depends on Him, yet He needs nothing;

He is the self-sustained, the One who holds the universe in balance.
He is the constant who does not change, while everything else is in flux.
No being exists without His sustaining power, and no force can exist without His permission.
In Him, we find the security that no material possession can provide; He is the one and only Sustainer.
When the world seems uncertain, remember: Al-Qayyum holds it all together.

"The Messenger of Allah cursed the one who consumes usury, the one who pays it, the one who writes it down, and the two who witness it, saying they are all the same.*" (Bukhari 2085)*

64. Al-Wajid الوَاجِدُ (The Perceiver)

The name "Al-Wājid" The Perceiver (The Finder) does not appear explicitly in the Qur'an. While the concept of Allah's finding or perceiving is mentioned in the Qur'an.

Key Verses: *Mentioned in 93:6-8*

"Did He not find you an orphan and give [you] refuge? And He found you lost and guided [you]. And He found you poor and made [you] self-sufficient." Surah Ad-Duha (93:6-8)

Al-Wajid; the One who finds all, who needs nothing yet holds everything; is the eternal seeker who never seeks, for all that is, flows from Him.

He is the source from which existence blooms, the light that illuminates every hidden corner.

He finds what others lose; what is lost in the world, He finds in His boundless wisdom.

Let the name of Al-Wajid remind you that what you seek is not beyond reach; it resides in His infinite rich.

Accept it with an open heart, and walk the path in trust and surrender

"Take advantage of five before five: Your youth before old age, your health before sickness, your wealth before poverty, your free time before busyness, and your life before death."
(Bukhari 5933)

65. Al-Majid المَاجِدُ (The Glorious, Most Honorable)

---

*The name **'Al-Majid'** (The Glorious, Most Honorable) is not explicitly mentioned in the Qur'an, but its meaning is reflected in the divine attributes described within it.*

Key Verses: *Mentioned in 11:73*

"Indeed, He is Praiseworthy and Glorious."
Surah Hud (11:73)

He is Glory itself; majestic in His beauty, splendor, and honor.

Al-Majid's presence illuminates every darkness; His magnificence cannot be described by words.

His honor is not of this world, but transcends it entirely.

No title can contain His greatness, no praise can encapsulate His worth.

When you stand before Him, you stand in the presence of the Most Honorable.

Al-Majid's glory is so vast that the heavens and the earth cannot contain it.

It is through His grace that we find honor; without Him, we are nothing but humble dust.

"Whoever does deeds to be seen by others, Allah will expose his intentions on the Day of Judgment."
(Bukhari 6499)

66. Al-Wahid الوَاحِدُ (The Only One)

*The name "Al-Wāḥid" The Only One is mentioned **15 times** in the **Qur'an**.*

***Key Verses**: Mentioned in 2:163, 39:4*

"And your god is one God. There is no deity [worthy of worship] except Him, the Entirely Merciful, the Especially Merciful." Surah Al-Baqarah (2:163)

Al-Wahid is the singularity of existence; the One from whom all things come.
All that exists, exists because of His will.
To Him belongs the essence of unity; everything is His creation, and yet He remains unmatched.
No partner shares His essence, no likeness compares.
In a world full of multiplicities, He is the one true reality.
The heart finds rest in the knowledge that He alone is worthy of worship, for He is the Only One.

There is no one like Him.

"There is nothing like unto Him" *[Quran 42:11]*

"Deeds are presented to Allah on Mondays and Thursdays, and I love for my deeds to be presented while I am fasting." *(Bukhari 1979)*

67. Al-Ahad الأَحَد (The Indivisible, The One)

*The name **"Al-Aḥad" The Indivisible, The One** is mentioned **once** in the Qur'an.*

Key Verses*: Mentioned in 112:1*

*"**Say: He is Allah, the One (Al-Aḥad)**" Surah Al-Ikhlas (112:1*

*He is the One, beyond counting, beyond division.
Al-Ahad is not a number, but the essence of unity itself.
Nothing divides Him, nothing shares in His existence; He is singular, complete, whole.
He is the One in whom all things find their origin, yet He stands alone, untouched by creation.
When you seek refuge in Him, know that you are seeking the One who can never be divided, never be diminished.
In your solitude, you are never truly alone, for He is always the One who is near.
Al-Ahad; there is none like Him, and there never will be.*

"The best prayer after the obligatory ones is the night prayer."
(Bukhari 1981)

68. As-Samad الصَّمَدُ (The Self-Sufficient, The Impregnable)

---

*The name **"As-Samād" The Self-Sufficient, The Impregnable** is mentioned **once** in the **Qur'an**.*

***Key Verses**: Mentioned in 112:2*

When all else crumbles, where do you turn? When the walls of your strength collapse, when friends drift like passing clouds, when even your own heart betrays you; **One remains.**

"Say: He is Allah, the One. Allah, the Self-Sufficient." (Quran 112:1-2)

He is the refuge of the weary, the anchor of the lost, the One who never falters, never abandons, never forgets.

As-Samad; the One who remains when all else fades.
All creation turns to Him, yet He depends on no one.
He is the Unshaken, the Eternal, the Absolute.
Time does not touch Him, nor does need diminish Him.
He is the sanctuary that never crumbles, the safe harbor in every storm.

When the world shifts beneath your feet, **As-Samad** remains firm.
Turn to Him, and in His presence, find the strength that never wavers.

"The most hated person to Allah is the one who is most argumentative."
(Bukhari 2457)

69. Al-Qadir القَادِرُ (The Omnipotent)

The name "Al-Qādir" The Omnipotent is mentioned **12 times** in the **Qur'an**.

Key Verses: Mentioned in 2:20, 85:8

"To Allah belongs the dominion of the heavens and the earth and whatever is within them. And He is over all things competent."
Surah Al-Ma'idah (5:120)

Nothing is beyond His reach, nothing escapes His power.
Al-Qadir is the One who commands the universe with a single word; "Be," and it is.

He is not bound by time, space, or any limitation, for His power is absolute.

The impossible is His creation, for He is the Creator of all things.

In every moment, He is the One who gives power, the One who takes it away.

When you feel powerless, remember that He is the Omnipotent, the One who grants strength to the weak.

In His will, all things are possible.

> *"Beware of envy, for envy consumes good deeds just as fire consumes wood."*
> *(Bukhari 32)*

70. Al-Muqtadir المُقْتَدِرُ (The Creator of All Power)

The name "Al-Muqtadir" The Creator of All Power is mentioned 2 times in the Qur'an.

Key Verses: *Mentioned in 82:8, 18:45*

"And present to them the example of the life of this world: [It is] like rain which We send down from the sky, and the vegetation of the earth mingles with it and [then] it becomes dry remnants, scattered by the winds. And Allah is ever, over all things, Perfect in Ability." Surah Al-Kahf (18:45)

He is the One who grants power, the One who takes it away.
Al-Muqtadir shapes the forces of nature with ease, commanding the world and the heavens.
There is no power but His power; all strength is a reflection of His will.
In His hands, the winds and the seas are but His instruments, obeying His command.
No force in the universe is independent of His will.
Al-Muqtadir's might is unmatched; what He decrees comes to pass without question.

He is the Creator of All Power, and it is through His grace that we are empowered.

"The generous person is close to Allah, close to Paradise, and far from Hellfire."
(Bukhari 2076)

71. Al-Muqaddim المُقَدِّمُ (The Expediter)

*The name **"Al-Muqaddim" The Expediter** is not explicitly mentioned verbatim in the Quran, it is derived from Allah's actions and attributes described in the Quran and Hadith.*

Key Verses: Mentioned in 56:10-11

"And the forerunners, the forerunners; those are the ones brought near [to Allah]." Surah Al-Waqi'ah (56:10-11)

He brings forward what He wills, placing each moment exactly where it belongs.

The journey of life may seem uncertain, but Al-Muqaddim knows when the time is right.

Do not fear what comes early; Al-Muqaddim is never mistaken in His timing.

He opens doors before we even realize we are ready. What arrives is meant to arrive, and what is given is meant to be received.

To trust Al-Muqaddim is to walk without hesitation, knowing He leads the way.

Nothing is rushed, yet nothing is delayed; everything unfolds in His wisdom.

*"Shall I inform you of the greatest sins?
Associating partners with Allah, disobeying
parents, and false testimony."*
(Bukhari 2654)

72. Al-Mu'akhkhir المُؤَخِّر (The Delayer)

The name "Al-Mu'akhkhir" The Delayer is not explicitly mentioned verbatim in the Quran; it is derived from Allah's actions and attributes described in the Quran and Hadith.

Key Verses: *Mentioned in 56:10-11*

"He will forgive you of your sins and delay you for a specified term." Surah Nuh (71:4)

What is held back is not lost, but reserved for its perfect time.

Delay is not denial; it is divine wisdom in action. When you feel left behind, remember that Al-Mu'akhkhir is only shaping a better path.

Patience is not waiting; it is trusting that His timing is never wrong.

He withholds only to give greater, removes only to replace with better.

Every pause, every moment of stillness, is a preparation for what is to come.

To surrender to Al-Mu'akhkhir is to surrender to a plan greater than your own.

"When you visit the sick, give him hope for a long life. This does not prevent what is destined, but it comforts the soul."
(Bukhari 5666)

73. Al-Awwal الأَوَّلُ (The First)

---

*The name "**Al-Awwal**" **The First** is mentioned **once** in the **Qur'an**.*

Key Verses: *Mentioned in 57:3*

Allah is Al-Awwal (The First) and Al-Akhir (The Last). He says:
"He is the First (Al-Awwal) and the Last (Al-Ākhir), the Manifest (Az-Zāhir) and the Hidden (Al-Bātin), and He is Knowing of all things." *Surah Al-Hadid (57:3)*

Allah is eternal. He existed before anything else and will remain after everything perishes. When you feel lost in the passage of time, find comfort in knowing that Allah is the First and the Last, the One who controls time itself.

He is the Alpha and the Omega, the Beginning and the End.

Before the beginning, He was.
All things emerge from His will, and nothing precedes Him.
Seek not origins in creation, for Al-Awwal is the true beginning of all things.
Every idea, every motion, every breath; all trace back to Him.
He was before time, and He remains beyond it.

No one is first except Al-Awwal, and no one leads except by His command.
Turn to Him at the start of all things, for all beginnings belong to Him.

"The one who recites the Quran beautifully and acts upon it will be with the noble angels."
(Bukhari 4937)

74. Al-Akhir الآخِرُ (The Last)

The name **"Al-Ākhir" The Last** is mentioned **1 time** in the **Qur'an**.

Key Verses: Mentioned in 57:3

When all fades, He remains.
The world is fleeting, but Al-Akhir is the eternal destination.
No ending is final, for every path returns to Him.
He is the last chapter of every story, the final answer to every question.
To seek Al-Akhir is to seek what never perishes.
Beyond every farewell, beyond every loss; He is there, waiting.
Anchor yourself in Al-Akhir, and you will never fear the end.

The Prophet taught us to say:

"You are the First, and there is nothing before You; You are the Last, and there is nothing after You..."
(Muslim 2713)

75. Az-Zahir الظَّاهِرُ (The Manifest)

*The name "Az-Zāhir" The Manifest is mentioned **1 time** in the **Qur'an**.*

Key Verses: *Mentioned in 57:3*

Signs of Him are everywhere, in the rise of the sun and the bloom of the flower.
He is not hidden, but revealed in every breath of creation.
The heart that seeks, finds; because Al-Zahir is never absent.
Look around you, and you will see the traces of His presence.
The universe is a mirror reflecting the beauty of Al-Zahir.
To recognize Him is to see beyond the surface, into the divine order of all things.
What seems ordinary, just because we used to His blessings, is but a doorway to the extraordinary.

"The glance is one of the poisoned arrows of Satan. Whoever lowers his gaze for Allah, He will replace it with sweetness of faith he will find in his heart."
(Bukhari 6226)

76. Al-Batin الْبَاطِنُ (The Hidden One, Knower of the Hidden)

*The name "Al-Bātin" The Hidden One, Knower of the Hidden is mentioned **one time** in the Qur'an.*

***Key Verses**: Mentioned in 57:3*

What is unseen is known to Him; no thought, no feeling, no secret escapes His awareness.
He is closer than the veins, yet beyond comprehension.
Al-Batin is in the silence, in the pauses, in the spaces between words.
Even when you feel alone, you are never unseen.
What is unknown to you is known to Him, and what is concealed is already written in His wisdom.
He hides so that we may seek, and in seeking, we may find.
To trust Al-Batin is to rest in the knowledge that nothing is truly lost.

"The truthful and trustworthy merchant will be with the prophets, the truthful, and the martyrs on the Day of Judgment."
(Bukhari 2088)

77. Al-Waali الوَالِي (The Sole Governor)

The name **"Al-Waalī"** (The Sole Governor) is not explicitly mentioned in the Qur'an, yet its essence and meaning are reflected throughout its verses.

Key Verses: Mentioned in 42:9

"Say, 'Who is Lord of the heavens and the earth?' Say, 'Allah.' Surah Ar-Ra'd (13:16)

He rules, not with tyranny, but with mercy and justice.
All things are under His command, and none can escape His care.
He is the true protector, the eternal guide.
Every kingdom rises and falls, but His authority never wavers.
Turn to Al-Waali, and you will find the safest refuge.
To submit to His governance is to be truly free.
No matter how great the power of man, all are subjects under Al-Waali's rule.

"Do not spy on one another."
(Bukhari 6064)

78. Al-Muta'ali المُتَعَالِي (The Self-Exalted)

---

*The name "Al-Mutā'alī" The **Supreme** is mentioned **once** in the **Qur'an**.*

Key Verses: *Mentioned in 13:9*

"Knower of the unseen and the witnessed, the Grand, the Exalted." Surah Ar-Ra'd (13:9)

None can reach His station, for He is above all things.
He is exalted beyond human limitations, yet closer than our own breath.
To know Al-Muta'ali is to stand in awe of His majesty.
No mind can grasp His greatness, yet the heart can feel His nearness.
He is beyond the heavens, yet within the whisper of the soul.
Bow before Al-Muta'ali, and you will find elevation in humility.
He is not distant, but above all imperfections.

"Allah helps His servant as long as the servant helps his brother."
(Bukhari 2442)

79. Al-Barr البَرُّ (The Source of All Goodness)

The name *"Al-Barr" The Source of All Goodness* is mentioned **once** in the *Qur'an*.

Key Verses: Mentioned in 52:28

"Indeed, we used to supplicate Him before. Indeed, it is He who is the Beneficent, the Merciful." Surah At-Tur (52:28)

Kindness, mercy, and love; all flow from Him.
His goodness is not conditional, but boundless.
Even in hardship, there is hidden kindness from Al-Barr.
The doors of goodness never close for those who turn to Him.
To believe in Al-Barr is to believe in a love that never falters.
He is gentle with His servants, even when they turn away.
What is good in this world is but a glimpse of His infinite generosity.

"Whoever believes in Allah and the Last Day, let him speak good or remain silent."
(Bukhari 6018)

80. At-Tawwab التَّوَّابُ (The Ever-Pardoning)

*The name "At-Tawwab" The Ever-Pardoning is mentioned **7 times** in the **Qur'an**.*

Key Verses: *Mentioned in 2:37, 4:16*

"Then Adam received from his Lord [some] words, and He accepted his repentance. Indeed, it is He who is the Accepting of Repentance, the Merciful." Surah Al-Baqarah (2:37)

No sin is too great, no heart too distant; At-Tawwab calls all back to Him.
Repentance is not just forgiveness; it is returning to the source of mercy.
He does not grow tired of forgiving, though we grow tired of seeking it.
Every step towards Him is met with an embrace of love.
At-Tawwab does not turn away those who seek Him, no matter how often they falter.
To ask for His pardon is to open the door to a new beginning.
The heart that repents is dear to Him, for He loves those who return.

The Prophet Muhammad Pbuh said:

There was a man who had killed 99 people.
He wanted to repent, so he went to a **monk** *and asked him,*
"Is there any repentance for me?"
The monk replied, "No!"
So the man **killed him too***, making it 100.*

Still seeking forgiveness, he went to a **scholar** *and asked the same question.*
The scholar said:

"Yes! Who can stand between you and repentance? But you are in a land of evil people. Go to such-and-such land; there are righteous people there. Worship Allah with them and never return to your old land."

So the man set out on his journey. While traveling, death overtook him.
The angels of mercy and punishment argued over him:

The angels of punishment said: "He never did any good."

The angels of mercy said: "He came seeking Allah's forgiveness!"

Then Allah sent an angel to judge between them. He ordered them to **measure the distance** *between the man's body and the two lands:*

If he was **closer to the righteous land***, he would be forgiven.*
If closer to the evil land, then not.

A Journey from Collapse to Clarity *Dr. Ashi Ezz*

*They measured and found he was just slightly closer
to the righteous land,
so Allah forgave him.*

Sahih al-Bukhari (no. 3470)

81. Al-Muntaqim المُنْتَقِمُ (The Just Requitor)

*The name "Al-Muntaqim" The Just Requitor is mentioned **1 time** in the **Qur'an**.*

***Key Verses**: Mentioned in 42:14*

"Indeed, you [disbelievers] and what you worship other than Allah are the firewood of Hell. You will be its inhabitants." *Surah Al-Furqan (25:19)*

Justice belongs to Him alone, and no deed escapes His sight.
He is neither hasty nor unjust, but when He requites, it is with perfect wisdom.
To those who oppress, He is the inescapable reckoning.
To those who suffer, He is the promise that no pain is forgotten.
Retribution in His hands is never cruel; it is balance restored.

Always keep the story of Pharaoh before your eyes as a timeless lesson and guide.

Pharaoh made this arrogant and blasphemous claim to elevate himself above all, even above God.

"And he said, 'I am your lord, the most high.'
Surah An-Nazi'at (79:24)

The Prophet Muhammad PBUH said:

"When Pharaoh was drowning, he said: 'I believe that there is no god except the One that the Children of Israel believe in.'
But Jibreel said:
'O Muhammad, if you could have seen me then! I was taking mud from the sea and stuffing it into Pharaoh's mouth, because I was afraid that the mercy of Allah might reach him.'"

Sahih Muslim, Book of Faith (no. 134)

Do you see it? Jibreel understands that the mercy of our Lord always surpasses His punishment in swiftness.

Fear not His justice, but fear the arrogance that denies it.
For every whisper of wrongdoing, Al-Muntaqim responds in His perfect measure.

82. Al-'Afuww العفو (The Supreme Pardoner)

---

*The name **"Al-'Afuww" The Supreme Pardoner** is mentioned **5 times** in the Qur'an.*

Key Verses: *Mentioned in 3:129, 4:99*

"Indeed, Allah is ever Pardoning ('Afuww), Forgiving (Ghafur)." *Surah An-Nisa (4:43)*

He erases, not just forgives.

Al-'Afuww does not remind you of your mistakes; He wipes them away as if they never were.

What burden do you carry, thinking it is too heavy for Him to remove?

He is not like men, who forgive with conditions; His mercy is absolute.

A single sincere tear can wash away years of wrongdoing in the eyes of Al-'Afuww.

Come to Him with shame, and leave with peace. For He does not hold on to your past, so why should you?

When Amr ibn al-'As came to accept Islam, he hesitated and said, "I will accept it, but I want my

past sins to be forgiven."
The Prophet (peace be upon him) replied:

"Do you not know that Islam wipes away what came before it? Hijrah wipes away what came before it, and Hajj wipes away what came before it?"

Sahih Muslim (Hadith 121)

83. Ar–Ra'uf الرَّءُوفَ (The Most Kind)

The name *"Ar-Ra'ūf"* **The Most Kind**
is mentioned **10 times** in the **Qur'an**.

Key Verses: *Mentioned in 2:143, 9:117*

"Do you not see that Allah has made subject to you whatever is on the earth and the ships which run through the sea by His command? And He restrains the sky from falling upon the earth, unless by His permission. Indeed, Allah, to the people, is Kind and Merciful."
Surah Al-Hajj (22:65)

His mercy is vast, but His kindness is even greater.
He does not just grant; He grants gently.
Every blessing is wrapped in His softness, every trial in His wisdom.
You are never tested beyond what you can bear, for Ar-Ra'uf knows the weight of your soul.
He does not only give what you need, but also what brings you joy.
Even in hardship, there are unseen mercies woven by Ar-Ra'uf's hands.
To recognize His kindness is to soften your own heart toward others.

This story always makes me pause and reflect and I know it happen to many of us.

Sometimes I walk a path and feel lost; unsure why I'm here. Frustrated, I once kicked a stone, only to realize I had freed a small creature trapped beneath it.

That moment hit me:

Even when I feel aimless, my presence may serve a purpose I can't see.

You might not always understand your journey, but trust Ar-Ra'uf's plan.

You may be here not just for yourself, but for someone else's moment of relief, growth, or guidance.

You're part of a perfect system; even when your vision is limited.

"You will not enter Paradise until you believe, and you will not believe until you love one another. Shall I guide you to something that will make you love one another? Spread greetings (Salam) among yourselves."
(Bukhari 12)

84. Malik-ul-Mulk مَالِكَ الْمُلْكِ (Master of the Kingdom, Owner of the Dominion)

---

*The exact phrase **"Malik-ul-Mulk"** Master of the Kingdom, Owner of the Dominion – is mentioned **1 time** in the **Qur'an**.*

Key Verses: *Mentioned in 3:26*

"You honor whom You will and You humble whom You will. In Your hand is [all] good. Indeed, You are over all things competent."
Surah Al-Imran (3:26)

All dominion belongs to Him, from the heavens to the earth, from the galaxies to the smallest grains of sand.
There is no ruler but Him, no kingdom but His, no authority that stands except by His will.
He is the master of the seen and unseen, of all that is known and unknown.
His throne is not just a symbol of power; it is the seat of ultimate sovereignty.

"His Throne extends o'er heavens and the Earth, Encompassing all realms, beyond their worth." Surah Al-Baqarah 2:255

He grants kingdoms, and He takes them away; no reign endures except by His decree.
His rule is perfect, His wisdom unparalleled, and His mercy boundless.
To Him, all returns, and His kingdom is eternal.

"The just will be seated on pulpits of light before Allah; those who are fair in their rulings and with their families."
(Bukhari 6724)

85. Dhul-Jalali Wal-Ikram ذُو الجَلَالِ وَالإِكْرَامِ

(Possessor of Glory and Honor)

---

*The exact phrase **"Dhul-Jalāli Wal-Ikram"** which translates to **"Possessor of Glory and Honor"**, is mentioned **2 times** in the **Qur'an**.*

Key Verses: *Mentioned in 55:27, 55:78*

"And there will remain the Face of your Lord, Owner of Majesty and Honor." Surah Ar-Rahman (55:27)

He is the possessor of glory, of majesty beyond imagination.
In His presence, even the mightiest of kings are but humble servants.
Dhul-Jalali Wal-Ikram does not just possess honor; He defines it.
He is the source of all nobility, all splendor, all dignity.
What is glorified in this world is merely a reflection of His infinite magnificence.
To know Him is to know true honor, and to seek Him is to seek the highest station.
In His mercy, there is glory; in His justice, there is

dignity. His honor lifts the humble and humbles the proud.

I yearn to behold Your divine face, O my Lord.

The Prophet Muhammad (peace be upon him) said:

"You will see your Lord on the Day of Resurrection just as you see this full moon ; you will have no difficulty in seeing Him."
(Sahih al-Bukhari, Hadith 7436; Sahih Muslim, Hadith 183)

86. Al-Muqsit المُقْسِطُ (The Just One)

---

*The name **"Al-Muqsiṭ"** **The Just One** is not explicitly mentioned verbatim in the Quran, it is derived from Allah's actions and attributes described in the Quran and Hadith.*

Key Verses: *Mentioned in 5:8, 3:18*

He is the perfect embodiment of justice, the one who sets right what is wrong.
Al-Muqsit does not favor one over another, for His justice is unbiased and absolute.
His judgment is the final word, for it is free from error and incompleteness.
He balances the scales, and in His hand, the world finds its rightful place.
Al-Muqsit's justice is not harsh; it is the restoration of what is due.
In His justice, the broken find healing, and the unjust find their reckoning.

A man came and sat in front of the Messenger of Allah (peace be upon him) and said:

"I have slaves who lie to me, betray me, and disobey me. I scold them and beat them. What is my position regarding them?"

The Prophet (peace be upon him) replied:

"On the Day of Judgment, their betrayal, disobedience, and lies will be weighed against your punishment of them. If your punishment matches their wrongdoing, it will be even; nothing for you, nothing against you. But if your punishment exceeds their wrongdoing, then retribution will be taken from you in their favor."

The man became deeply shaken. He stood and began crying and calling out in distress.

The Prophet (peace be upon him) then said:

"Do you not read the words of Allah:
'And We shall set up the scales of justice on the Day of Resurrection, so that no soul will be wronged in anything. And even if it be the weight of a mustard seed, We will bring it forth...'"
(Surah Al-Anbiya 21:47)

The man then said:

"O Messenger of Allah, I find no better solution for myself or them than to free them all. I make you witness that they are all free."

Narrated by Ahmad (in Musnad Ahmad) and al-Tirmidhi

87. Al-Jami' الجَامِعُ (The Gatherer, the Uniter)

The name "Al-Jāmi'" The Gatherer, The Uniter is not explicitly mentioned verbatim in the Quran, it is derived from Allah's actions and attributes described in the Quran and Hadith.

Key Verses: Mentioned in 3:9

"Our Lord, surely You will gather the people for a Day about which there is no doubt. Indeed, Allah does not fail in His promise."
Surah Al-Imran (3:9)

He unites what has been torn apart, brings together what has been scattered.
Al-Jami' gathers souls, hearts, and worlds into His embrace, nothing drift from His will.
He does not just unite the parts; He makes them whole again.
All things, in the end, return to Him, and in His presence, there is no division.
The separated are reunited, the lost found, the broken made whole.
Even in the face of great distance, He reconnects all.
To be in His presence is to know that nothing is ever truly lost; He gathers all into His mercy.

One of the most important gatherings for Muslims is the one around the Hawd in the judgement day

The Messenger of Allah (peace be upon him) said:

"I will be at the Hawd (the Pond) before you. Whoever comes to it will drink from it, and whoever drinks from it will never feel thirst again. People I know and who know me will come to me, but a barrier will be placed between me and them."

And in another narration:

"Your meeting with me is at the Hawd (the Pond)."

Sahih al-Bukhari, Hadith 6582; Sahih Muslim, Hadith 2290.

88. Al-Ghaniyy الغَنِيِّ (The Self-Sufficient, the Wealthy)

The name *"Al-Ghaniyy" The Self-Sufficient, The Wealthy* is mentioned **18 times** in the **Qur'an**.

Key Verses: Mentioned in 2:263, 6:133

The hands of humanity are always outstretched; seeking, yearning, grasping. Yet He, Al-Ghani, the Self-Sufficient, has never needed nor will He ever need.

The kingdom of the heavens and the earth belongs to Him, yet He asks for nothing.

The beggar and the king both bow before His might, for all are impoverished except He who is eternally rich.

"O mankind, you are those in need of Allah, while Allah is the Free of need, the Praiseworthy." (Quran 35:15)

The moment we realize our dependence on Him is the moment we taste true freedom.

He needs no one and nothing, yet He grants to all. Al-Ghaniyy's wealth is beyond what the mind can fathom; His sufficiency, beyond what any heart can comprehend.

He is not dependent on anything, yet everything is dependent on Him.

Wealth, true wealth, is not in possessions but in His nearness.

Al-Ghaniyy does not give from what He has, but from what He is; limitless and abundant.

You are rich only because He allows you to be; you are sufficient only because He provides.

When you are in need, it is His wealth you seek, for He is the source of every blessing.

89. Al-Mughni المُغْنِي (The Enricher)

The name "Al-Mughni" The Enricher is not explicitly mentioned verbatim in the Quran, it is derived from Allah's actions and attributes described in the Quran and Hadith.

Key Verses: Mentioned in 65:2-3

"And that it is He who enriches and suffices."
Surah An-Najm (53:48)

He enriches not just your material needs, but your soul's deepest longings.
Al-Mughni does not merely fill; He makes full.
From Him flows an unceasing stream of richness that saturates every corner of existence.
To be enriched by Him is to be blessed in ways both seen and unseen.
He does not just give you wealth; He enriches your heart with peace, your mind with wisdom.
The richness He provides goes beyond gold and silver; it is the wealth of spirit, of love, of grace.
Even when your pockets are empty, Al-Mughni can fill you with treasures that cannot be counted.

Just don't be like that man; he thought his success was all his doing,

"*I was only given it (this wealth) because of knowledge I have.*"

Surah Al-Qasas (28:78)

forgetting that it was a test, not a trophy. Arrogance blinded him to the Source of all blessings.

So, walk with gratitude, not pride; for what you have is a trust, not a triumph.

90. Al-Mani' المَانِع (The Withholder)

The name *"Al-Mani'" The Withholder* is not explicitly mentioned verbatim in the Quran, it is derived from Allah's actions and attributes described in the Quran and Hadith.

Key Verses: Mentioned in 35:2, 6:17

"And if Allah should touch you with adversity, there is no remover of it except Him; and if He touches you with good; then He is over all things competent." Surah Al-An'am (6:17)

He withholds not to harm, but to protect. What He does not give is never a loss, but a mercy. Al-Mani' keeps from you what would harm your soul, what would pull you further from His light. He withholds, but never out of malice; His withholding is always for your own good. Trust in His wisdom, for He knows what you truly need, and what would only lead you astray. What He keeps from you is not lost; it is simply not yet time, or it is not yours to bear.

Don't act like you hold the reins of destiny; even the Prophet was told:
"You have no say in the matter."

Surah Aal-Imran (3:128)

So, trust the One who sees what we can't, and leave the outcomes to the All-Knowing.

To accept His withholding is to trust that He knows best and that His plan for you is greater than your own.

91. Ad-Darr الضَّارُّ (The Distresser)

---

*The name **"Ad-Dhārr" The Distresser** is not explicitly mentioned verbatim in the Quran, it is derived from Allah's actions and attributes described in the Quran and Hadith..*

Key Verses: *Mentioned in 6:17*

"If Allah should afflict you with harm, none can remove it except Him." *Surah Al-An'am (6:17)*

In every trial lies a lesson, for Ad-Darr is not a force of destruction but of transformation.
He does not harm for the sake of harm; He distresses to awaken, to refine.
The storm may shake you, but it is only to cleanse you.
No difficulty is meaningless, for even in distress, His mercy is found.
When all seems lost, know that Ad-Darr holds the key to your healing.
Every wound inflicted by the world is an opportunity to seek His comfort and grow.

Read The Story of the Garden in Surah Al-Qalam (68:17–33)

*Allah tells us about a group of brothers who inherited a beautiful, fruitful garden from their righteous father. Their father used to **give a portion of the harvest to the poor**, as was his duty and act of gratitude to Allah.*

*But **after his death**, the sons **grew selfish and greedy**. They said to one another:*

"Let's harvest it early in the morning before the poor come, so we won't have to give them anything."

*They made a secret plan to **prevent the needy from benefiting** from the garden. But while they were asleep, **Allah sent a calamity**, and **the garden was burned to ashes**.*

When they arrived the next morning, they were shocked and said:

"Surely, we have gone the wrong way!"
Then they realized:
"No, this is it; our garden is gone!"

Eventually, they admitted their wrongdoing and said:

"Woe to us! We were truly wrongdoers."

Do not despair in hardship; it is merely a prelude to His relief.

"There should be neither harming (darar) nor reciprocating harm (dirar)."
(Bukhari 32)

92. An-Nafi' النَّافِعُ (The Propitious, the Benefactor)

The name "An-Nāfi'" The Propitious, the Benefactor does not appear explicitly in the Qur'an as an exact name of Allah. While the concept of Allah being the benefactor, the source of benefit, or the one who gives benefits, is mentioned in various forms, the specific name "An-Nāfi'" is not directly stated in the Qur'an.

Key Verses: Mentioned in

"If Allah touches you with harm, none can remove it except Him. And if He intends good for you, none can repel His bounty." Surah Yunus (10:107)

He is the source of every favor, the giver of every blessing.
What He bestows upon you is beyond measure, far more than you deserve.
An-Nafi' does not give out of need, but out of infinite generosity.
He enriches the soul before He enriches the body, bringing true prosperity to those who trust Him.
Every moment of joy in your life is a gift from An-

*Nafi', who showers His kindness with no limit.
Ask from Him, but be assured that He will always give more than you imagined.
His favor is not bound by time or space, for He is the Sustainer of all things.*

Check this out

During the time of the Prophet Muhammad (peace be upon him) in Medina, there was a well called Bi'r Rumah (the Well of Rumah). It was one of the few sources of water in the area, but it was owned by a man who sold water for a high price, making it difficult for many Muslims to access it, especially the poor.

The Prophet (peace be upon him), seeing the hardship of his people, said:

"Whoever buys the Well of Rumah and gives water freely to the Muslims, will be rewarded with a well in Paradise."

(Hadith in Al-Tirmidhi and others)

Uthman's Response

When Uthman ibn Affan (RA), one of the wealthiest and most generous companions, heard this, he went to the owner of the well and offered to buy it. The man refused to sell it entirely, so Uthman proposed a deal:

He would buy half of the well, meaning on alternate days, Uthman would provide free water to the people.

The owner agreed. But soon, people only came on Uthman's day, since it was free. Seeing his profits drop, the owner offered to sell the other half, and Uthman bought it completely, donating it as a public resource.

Be like Uthman and reflect your Lord name in you

93. An-Nur النُّورُ (The Light)

The name "An-Nūr" some write it An-Noor" The Light is mentioned 1 time in the Qur'an.

Key Verses: *Mentioned in 24:35*

Allah is **An-Noor**; The Light.

"Allah is the Light of the heavens and the earth." *(Quran 24:35)*

His light is more than what the eyes perceive; it is the glow of truth, the clarity of guidance, the radiance that lifts the soul from shadows. Just as dawn dispels the night, Allah's light banishes ignorance, doubt, and sin.

When you seek direction, turn to **An-Noor**, the One who illuminates hearts and minds. The Prophet Muhammad (peace be upon him) prayed:

"O Allah, place light in my heart, light in my hearing, light in my sight, and light in my soul."

True light is not just seen; it is felt. It awakens the spirit, clears the fog of confusion, and leads to tranquility.

*To be near **An-Noor** is to be bathed in brilliance.
His light does not merely shine; it transforms.
It turns hesitation into certainty, fear into peace.
The heart that seeks His radiance will never be lost.*

*When the world feels dim, seek His light. **An-Noor** is the light of the heavens, the earth, and the soul; no darkness can ever extinguish it.*

94. Al-Hadi الهَادِي (The Guide)

The name **"Al-Hādī"** **The Guide** is mentioned **12 times** in the **Qur'an**.

Key Verses: Mentioned in 22:54, 25:31

"And thus We have made for every prophet an enemy from among the criminals. But sufficient is your Lord as a guide and a helper." Surah Al-Furqan (25:31)

He does not leave you wandering; He is the beacon in the wilderness.
Al-Hadi knows the path you must take, even when you do not.
His guidance is subtle but unmistakable, gentle but certain.
When you feel lost, know that Al-Hadi is closer than your breath, ready to direct you.
His wisdom is perfect, His signs abundant. It is not the absence of signs, but the absence of awareness that causes us to stray.
Turn your heart toward Him, and He will show you the way.
To walk under His guidance is to walk in peace, no matter the obstacles ahead.

Abu Sufyan once stood firm in opposition; a leader of resistance against Islam.

But when truth dawned on his heart, he embraced faith and dignity.

His journey reminds us: Even the fiercest adversary can become a valuable ally when guided by truth.

Never write off a soul; hearts are in the hands of the Most Merciful."

95. Al-Badi البَدِيعُ (Incomparable Originator)

*The name "Al-Bādiʿ" The Incomparable Originator is mentioned **two times** in the Qur'an.*

***Key Verses**: Mentioned in 2:117, 6:101*

"Originator of the heavens and the earth. When He decrees a matter, He only says to it, 'Be,' and it is." Surah Al-Baqarah (2:117)

He creates without a model, and everything He creates in perfection.
Al-Badi's creations are born from His will alone, each a miracle of originality.

"There is no creature on the earth or bird that flies with its wings except that they are communities like you. We have not neglected anything in the Book. Then to their Lord they will be gathered."
(Surah Al-An'am 6:38)

Every leaf, every star, every breath is a testimony to His unmatched power to create from nothing.

Al-Badi invites you to witness the beauty in the ever-changing, ever-renewing creation around you.

In a world that seeks sameness, He brings forth what is unlike anything that came before.

To ponder His creations is to witness the grandeur of Al-Badi, the master of beginnings.

96. Al-Baqi الْبَاقِي (The Ever-Surviving)

*The name "Al-Bāqī" The Ever-Surviving does **not** appear as an exact word in the Qur'an. However, the concept of Allah's eternal and everlasting existence is mentioned in several verses.*

Key Verses: Mentioned in 55:27

"Everyone upon the earth will perish, and there will remain the Face of your Lord, Owner of Majesty and Honor." Surah Ar-Rahman (55:26-27)

The world fades, kingdoms fall, and bodies decay, but Al-Baqi endures.

He is the eternal presence, the foundation that will never crumble.

Wherever you search for permanence, you will find it only in Al-Baqi.

The world's illusions of eternity are fleeting, but He remains unchanged.

Trust in Him, for no loss is permanent when you are anchored in the Ever-Surviving.

In every ending, there is a reminder that He alone is the everlasting reality.

The Messenger of Allah said:
"When a person dies, his deeds come to an end except for three: an ongoing charity, beneficial knowledge, or a righteous child who prays for him."

97. Al-Warith الوَارِثُ (The Inheritor)

The name **"Al-Wārith" The Inheritor** is mentioned **3 times** in the **Qur'an**.

Key Verses: Mentioned in 19:40, 15:23, 28:58

Allah is Al-Warith (The Inheritor). He says:
"Indeed, We inherit the earth and whoever is on it, and to Us they will be returned." *(Quran 19:40)*

Everything in this world is temporary. The wealth, the power, the possessions; all of it will fade away, and only Allah will remain.

When you reflect on this name, you are reminded to focus on the eternal rather than the temporary. Let go of what you cannot keep, and hold on to what you cannot lose: your faith, your deeds, and your connection to Allah.

Everything you cherish will one day leave your hands, but Al-Warith remains the rightful owner of all.
He is the ultimate inheritor, the one who claims what is truly His.
All things in the world are entrusted to you temporarily; when you pass, they return to their

true owner.
In every loss, there is the truth of Al-Warith: nothing is ever truly lost, but only passed on.
What you think you own belongs to Him, and He allows you to use it for a while.
In Him lies the eternal inheritance, the treasures that never fade.
Those who seek His inheritance will find a wealth far greater than anything the world can offer.

Your life may end, but your impact doesn't have to. Plant seeds that keep growing, in charity, knowledge, and righteous legacy.

"Allah hates for you three things: Gossip, begging, and wasting wealth."
(Muslim 1715)

98. As-Sabur الصَّبُورُ (The Forbearing)

*The name **"As-Sabūr" The Forbearing** is not explicitly mentioned verbatim in the Quran, but it is derived from Allah's attributes and actions described in the Quran and Hadith.*

Key Verses: *Mentioned in 16:127*

"And be patient, [O Muhammad], and your patience is not but through Allah. And do not grieve over them and do not be in distress over what they conspire." Surah An-Nahl (16:127)

He delays punishment for those who transgress, giving them countless chances to turn back, seek forgiveness, and mend their ways.

His patience is beyond human comprehension; it is not born of need or weakness but is a manifestation of His boundless wisdom and mercy.

He waits patiently as you struggle, giving you chance to come back.
In His patience is a lesson: to endure, to persevere, and to trust that His timing is perfect.

every trial has a purpose and that ease will follow hardship.

Imitate His forbearance, for in it lies peace beyond understanding.

The Battle of Uhud was a fierce and painful moment in early Islamic history.

Amid the chaos, the Prophet Muhammad (peace be upon him) was severely wounded:

His face was cut,

His tooth was broken,

Blood flowed from his forehead,

He fell into a pit, and his companions rushed to protect him.

Even when his face was wounded and his people betrayed his command, the Prophet didn't respond with anger; he responded with prayer:

"O Allah, forgive my people, for they do not know."
(Sahih al-Bukhari)

99. Ar-Rashid الرَّشِيدُ (The Guide, Infallible Teacher, and Knower)

The name "Ar-Rashid" The Guide, Infallible Teacher, and Knower does not appear explicitly in the Qur'an as an exact name of Allah while the concept is there.

Key Verses: *Mentioned in 72:10*

"And we do not know [therefore] whether evil is intended for those on earth or whether their Lord intends for them a right course."
Surah Al-Jinn (72:10)

He does not just show the way; He teaches you how to walk it.

Ar-Rashid does not leave you in confusion; He clarifies every doubt with perfect wisdom.

The one who seeks His guidance is never misled, for He is the infallible teacher.

His knowledge encompasses all things, past, present, and future, and from it, He imparts the wisdom you need.

When you are in need of direction, turn to Ar-Rashid, and you will find your path illuminated.

His teachings do not just inform; they transform.

In the presence of Ar-Rashid, every question is answered, every uncertainty resolved.

"*Lying leads to wickedness, and wickedness leads to the Fire.*"
(Muslim 2607)

Narrated by 'Umar ibn al-Khattab:

"One day, while we were sitting with the Messenger of Allah (*pbuh*), a man with pure white clothing and jet-black hair appeared. He showed no signs of travel, yet none of us recognized him. He sat close to the Prophet (*pbuh*), knees touching his, and placed his hands on his thighs. He said:

1. Question about Islam:

'O Muhammad, tell me about Islam.'
The Prophet (*pbuh*) replied:
"Islam is to testify that there is no god but Allah and Muhammad is His Messenger, establish prayer, pay Zakat, fast Ramadan, and perform Hajj if you can."
The man said: "You have spoken truthfully."

2. Question about Iman (Faith):

'Now, tell me about Iman.'
The Prophet (*pbuh*) replied:
"Iman is to believe in Allah, His angels, His books, His messengers, the Last Day, and divine decree (Qadr);both its good and bad."
The man said: "You have spoken truthfully."

3. Question about Ihsan (Spiritual Excellence):

'Now, tell me about Ihsan.'
The Prophet (*pbuh*) replied:
"Ihsan is to worship Allah as if you see Him, for though you do not see Him, He sees you."

4. Question about the Hour (Day of Judgment):

'Tell me about the Hour.'
The Prophet (*pbuh*) replied:
"The one questioned knows no more than the questioner."
The man then asked: "Then tell me of its signs."
The Prophet (*pbuh*) said:
"The slave-girl will give birth to her mistress, and barefoot, destitute shepherds will compete in constructing tall buildings."

The man left, and after a while, the Prophet (*pbuh*) asked:
"O 'Umar, do you know who the questioner was?"
I said: 'Allah and His Messenger know best.'
He said: 'That was Jibril (Gabriel). He came to teach you your religion.'"

(Sahih Muslim 55, Book 1: Faith)

Epilogue

As we reach the end of our journey through the Beautiful Names of our Lord, I'm filled with awe at the profound insights we've encountered along the way. In this closing chapter, I'd love to share a few powerful reflections that have stood out; lessons that have left a lasting imprint on my heart, and I hope will inspire yours as well.

Reflection 1: Don't be Among the Blinds People

Look around, seeker; do you not see? The mountain stands in silent remembrance, the river sings praises as it rushes toward its destiny. Every leaf that quivers in the wind, every drop of rain that kisses the earth; each is a verse, a signs letter for all.

Allah reminds us:

"And among His signs is that He shows you lightning, [causing] fear and hope, and He sends down from the sky water and gives life thereby to the earth after its lifelessness." (Quran 30:24)

The One who revives the dead land can also revive the dead heart. Are we listening? Are we seeing?

"Is there a god with Allah? No! But they are a people who ascribe equals [to Him]." Surah An-Naml (27:60)

Reflection 2: Heavenly Repetition: The Hidden Patterns of the Lord names in Quran

If we check the frequency of Allah names in Quran; we will be so surprised. It is a rain of knowledge, an ocean of forgiveness and mercy. Check the frequency table below

ARABIC NAME	ENGLISH MEANING	FREQUENCY IN QURAN
ALLAH	The One True God	2699
AL-ALIM	The All-Knowing	157
AR-RAHIM	The Most Gracious	114
AL-HAKIM	The All-Wise	97
AL-AZEEZ	The Almighty	92
AL-GHAFUR	The Ever-Forgiving	91
AR-RAHMAN	The All-Merciful	57
AS-SAMI'	The All-Hearing	45
AL-KHABIR	The All-Aware	45
AL-BASIR	The All-Seeing	42

Let us begin with a discerning perspective.

- The name "**Allah**" dominates the Quran; appearing **2699 times**, a towering presence above all else.

A clear message unfolds:
The Quran's heart is not an attribute, but Allah Himself.

The core message of the Quran is **Tawhid**, the absolute Oneness of God; a truth that calls to the depths of the human soul. This sacred Oneness is incomplete without **Ikhlas** (الإخلاص), or sincerity, which breathes life into faith itself. While not one of the "Five Pillars," Ikhlas stands as a quiet yet mighty foundation, urging us to strip away all pretense and worldly desire. It beckons us to act purely for the sake of Allah, not for show, not for praise, not for fleeting gains.

In its essence, Ikhlas transforms worship into a heartfelt connection with the Divine, reminding us of the profound purity of truly living for Allah alone.

For Whom Are You Working?"

It's not about what you do.

It's about for whom you do it.

Brothers and sisters, listen closely

No matter what you do, no matter how great your efforts,

if your work is not for Allah,

there is no good in it.

Oh, the tragedy of a corrupted intention!

How many towering deeds have crumbled to dust because the heart was not pure?

The Messenger of Allah warned us;

the first to be thrown into the fire on the Day of Judgment

will not be the disbeliever,

not the oppressor,

but a man who gave in charity,

a man who recited the Qur'an,

and a man who died a martyr.

Yes; people who outwardly served Islam,

but inwardly, they only sought the applause of others,

the admiration of the crowd,

the praise of the people.

They wanted the world to see them, not Allah.

If Allah is not your goal,

every building you raise is already in ruins.

If Allah is not your destination,

every road you travel leads only to loss.

If you do not purify your heart for His sake,

then do not exhaust yourself;

for all that effort, all that striving, will vanish into nothing.

Purify your heart.

Fix your intention.

Make Allah your only audience, your only desire, your only aim.

And know;

even the smallest deed, when done sincerely for Him,

is greater than mountains of deeds done for the eyes of men.

So, ask yourself today:

For whom are you working?

For whom are you living?

And for whom do you seek to be remembered?

Return to Allah with a heart full of sincerity,

before it is too late.

Check this

A man came to the Prophet (peace and blessings be upon him) and said: "O Messenger of Allah! What do you think of a

man who fights seeking reward and fame, what does he get?" The Messenger of Allah (peace and blessings be upon him) said: "He gets nothing." Then he (the man) repeated it three times, and the Prophet said: "Allah only accepts deeds that are done sincerely for His sake alone."

Our Lord is far above any act lacking sincerity, accepting only the purest intentions offered with devotion and love.

Before mercy, before wisdom; first, the One, the Unique, the Ever-Present.

Faith begins not with admiring God's qualities, but with surrendering to His existence, His Oneness, His nearness.

- **Al-'Alim (العليم) – The All-Knowing (157 times):**
  Knowledge precedes action.
  God's mercy, wisdom, and even might are not random; they spring from infinite knowledge. For us, too: knowledge must lead the way ; not prideful knowledge, but sincere, searching truth.

- **Ar-Rahim (الرحيم) – The Most Gracious (114 times):**
  Mercy shapes the universe.
  After existence and knowledge, comes mercy; not vengeance, not dominance.
  And remarkably, mercy outweighs might,

appearing **twice** as often as "The Almighty" (Al-Azeez).
Love, before fear, anchors creation.

- **Al-Hakim (الحكيم) – The All-Wise (97 times):**
  Wisdom is knowledge applied justly.
  Not all knowledge uplifts. Only wisdom elevates knowledge to justice, fairness, and compassion.
  The Quran whispers:
  "Know deeply, but live wisely."

- **Al-Azeez (العزيز) – The Almighty (92 times):**
  Power is framed by mercy and wisdom.
  In the Divine order, might follows knowledge, mercy, and wisdom.
  Without wisdom, power corrupts; without mercy, power destroys.
  But with Allah, might is the servant of mercy.

- **Al-Ghafur (الغفور) – The Ever-Forgiving (91 times):**
  Forgiveness crowns might.
  Despite omnipotence, God chooses to forgive. For humanity; ever stumbling, ever yearning; this is the grandest comfort:
  Our Creator's hand is always extended in forgiveness.

- **Ar-Rahman (الرحمن) – The All-Merciful (57 times):**

Mercy without bounds.
Rahman envelops all beings; believer and rebel alike; with a mercy that nourishes existence itself.
It is the sun that shines on all faces.

Presence Over Distance:

As-Sami' (السميع), **Al-Basir (البصير)**, and **Al-Khabir (الخبير)**; appearing **42–45 times** each;
paint a vivid picture:
God is intimately near.
He hears every whisper, sees every tear, knows every hidden sorrow.
No soul is unseen; no prayer is unheard.

And if we looked Deeper:

- **Order Matters:**
  The Quran emphasizes mercy, knowledge, and forgiveness far more than wrath or punishment.
  The emotional climate of revelation is not terror, but **hope**, **love**, and **return**.

- **Balance Among Attributes:**
  God's qualities intertwine:
  Knowledge with Wisdom.
  Might with Mercy.
  Presence with Forgiveness.
  For the believer, these are not distant concepts, but a blueprint for living.

- **A Spiritual Secret:**
  "Allah" is mentioned so vastly more than any

attribute because:
Knowing Allah Himself transforms the heart.
When you know *Him*, trust naturally follows. Hope blooms.
Fear finds its rightful place; not as despair, but awe.
The goal is not merely to admire mercy or fear might, but to be *drawn near* to Allah in His fullness.

Gazing at this table of divine frequencies is like gazing into a mirror of heaven's priorities:
Existence before attributes.
Mercy before might.
Wisdom before decree.
Forgiveness before judgment.

The Prophet Muhammad (peace and blessings be upon him) said:
"Indeed, Allah does not sleep, and it is not befitting for Him to sleep. He lowers the scales and raises them. The deeds of the night are taken up to Him before the deeds of the day, and the deeds of the day before the deeds of the night. His veil is Light. If He were to remove it, the radiance of His Face would burn everything of His creation that His sight reaches."
Narrated by Muslim (179).

In every breath of the Quran, the soul hears a call:
Know your Lord. Love your Lord. Walk in His light.

Subhan'Allah ; Glory be to the One who revealed Himself with such perfect harmony.

Now, let us draw words cloud from this table and see what it also reflects.

O seeker, look! Not with your eyes, but with your heart.

This is no mere gathering of words;

it is a garden of light, a sky of whispers,

a river of meanings flowing from the Source.

See how some names rise, towering like mountains;

The All-Knowing, The Most Gracious, The Ever-Forgiving.

And others glow like hidden fireflies;

The All-Hearing, The All-Seeing, The All-Aware.

This is no accident.

The Beloved speaks in rhythms, in echoes, in waves.

The names most spoken are the names most reflected and impressed.

For what is this world but a mirror, reflecting Him?

The All-Knowing Watches,

The Most Gracious Embraces

Before you spoke, He knew.

Before you sought, He had already written.

The pen does not hesitate, nor does the ink run dry.

The All-Knowing (Al-'Alim), the word stands grand,

for knowledge is the first pillar of existence.

And mercy? Ah, mercy is the sky above all things!
The Most Gracious (Ar-Rahman) spreads vast,
for love does not measure, it simply pours.
Like the sun, it warms all;
the grateful and the heedless alike.
Even when you turn away, He shades you still.

The Ever-Forgiving Waits, The Almighty Holds
O heart heavy with regret, do you not see?
The Ever-Forgiving (Al-Ghaffar) repeats, again and again;
for every fall is met with an ocean,
for every sin, there are waves of return.
He does not tire of forgiving,
but do you tire of seeking?
He lifts the worlds, holds the stars, both His hands are right.

One Name, Many Doors
The Name you call is the door you knock upon.

Do you seek guidance? Call upon Al-Hadi, The Guide.

Do you seek healing? Whisper Ash-Shafi, The Healer.

Do you seek justice? Stand before Al-Adl, The Just.

But ah! They do not stand alone;

they weave into one another, like stars forming constellations,

like threads of a single tapestry.

The All-Knowing guides; The Most Merciful to forgive.

The Almighty strengthens; The Ever-Forgiving to heal.

The All-Seeing watches as; The Most Gracious pours love.

A Word Cloud? No, a Map to the Divine!

O seeker, do not just see; listen.

They are signs for us, echoes of eternity.

So, tell me, beloved, which name calls to your soul today?

Which door will you knock upon?

For every name is a key, waiting in your hands.

Turn it, open it;

and step into the Light.

Reflection 3: The Loftiness of Allah

Look up to the heavens, where galaxies swirl in silent majesty. Beyond all that we can see, beyond all that we can comprehend, there is One who reigns above all;

- **Al-A'la,**
- **Al-Ali,**
- **Al-Muta'ali.**

The Most High, The Exalted, The Self-Exalted.

His greatness is not measured by distance, nor by height, but by His absolute and unmatched supremacy. Come, let us embark on a journey to understand the beauty of these divine names.

Look around you. Everything you witness is bound by limits. The mountains may touch the sky, but they crumble with time. The stars may burn with brilliance, but they, too, will fade. Yet, there is One whose greatness neither wanes nor wearies:

"And He is not weary of preserving them, and He is the Most High, the Most Great." (Quran 2:255)

"Glorify the name of your Lord, the Most High." (Quran 87:1)

> "**Knower of the unseen and the seen, the Great, the Most High.**" (Quran 13:9)

This loftiness is not spatial; it is a loftiness of power, knowledge, and authority. It is the loftiness of the One who holds existence in His grasp, yet nothing can grasp Him.

Beyond human grasp, beyond the highest heavens, lies the throne of the Almighty. His knowledge pervades everything. His presence is above all, yet closer to you than your own breath.

Who is the One to whom all things rise?

He is **Dhul Ma'arij (The Possessor of Ascents)**, as the Quran declares:

> "**The angels and the Spirit ascend to Him in a day, the measure of which is fifty thousand years.**" (Quran 70:4)

Your prayers, your hopes, your sighs of despair; they all ascend to Him. Every deed rises like a whisper to the heavens. What then, will you send forth?

If you knew the weight of a single word of praise upon the scales, your tongue would never cease to glorify Him.

> "**And glorify the name of your Lord, the Most Great.**" (Quran 56:74)

Say it often: **"O Possessor of Majesty and Honor."**

"Yā Dhā al-Jalāli wal-Ikrām"

And remember this,

Pride is His cloak and greatness is His robe

Avoid being misguided or deceived like the illusioned fragile human below.

There once was a king who proclaimed:

"I am your Lord, the Most High." (Quran 79:24)

He was Pharaoh, and he drowned in the very waters over which he once claimed dominion. Iblis refused to bow, and he was cast out. The pattern of history is clear: arrogance is the path to ruin.

Umar ibn Al-Khattab, a man who once struck fear into the hearts of his enemies, came to understand:

"We were the most humiliated people, then Allah honored us with Islam. If we seek honor through anything other than what Allah honored us with, He will humiliate us."

Greatness belongs only to the One who needs no recognition. To seek it elsewhere is to chase shadows.

Reflection 4: His is Al-Kafi "The Sufficient One"

Is there any refuge other than in Him? When the world turns dark, when the weight of sorrow bends your back, when no hand reaches out to catch you; He is there.

"Is not Allah sufficient for His servant?"
(Quran 39:36)

Al-Kafi, the Sufficient, is the answer to every whispered prayer, the solace in every silent tear. The heart that truly knows Him needs nothing else.

Check this immense reward of simple Dhikr (Remembrance)

a small action with a huge eternal reward, this is common in islam.

The Messenger of Allah (peace and blessings be upon him) said:

"Whoever performs ghusl (full washing) on Friday, then goes early to the mosque, walking and not riding, sits close to the Imam, listens attentively and does not engage in idle talk ; for every step he takes, he will have the reward of a year's worth of deeds: the reward of fasting it and praying Qiyam (night prayer) during it."

Reported by Ahmad, Abu Dawood, and al-Tirmidhi; authenticated by Al-Albani.

The Messenger of Allah (peace and blessings be upon him) passed by Abu Huraira while he was planting a plant, and said:

"Shall I not tell you of something better to plant? Say: Subḥān Allāh, Al-ḥamdu lillāh, Lā ilāha illā Allāh, and Allāhu Akbar; for each one, a tree will be planted for you in

Paradise." Reported by Ibn Mājah (Hadith 3790), and authenticated by Al-Albani.

The All-Sufficient and Supreme,
Is that He has no need for creation's esteem.
Our prayers and worship add not to His might,
Nor do they take from His infinite light.

Yet for us, these acts are a gift and a guide,
They cleanse the soul and keep the heart tied.
Submission to Him is our spirit's release,
Through worship we find fulfillment and peace.

Allah, *Al-Kafi*, in perfection remains,
Our devotion is ours; to reap the gains.

With Him, you will never stray;

Without Him, you're lost along the way.

Reflection 5: All Bow to Him

What is power, if not the command that brought existence into being? Allah's power is not limited by the laws of physics or human understanding. He is **Al-Qadir**, the One who decrees and it becomes. He is **Al-Muqtadir**, the Supreme who holds all dominion, and **Al-Qahhar**, the Subduer before whom all creation humbles itself.

"Is not He who created the heavens and the earth able to create the likes of them? Yes,

and He is the Creator, the Knowing." (Quran 36:81)

No force can resist His will, no entity can challenge His decree.

Reflection 6: The Illusion of Death

Death is not the end; it is a return to Allah, **Al-Muhyi** (The Giver of Life). The Prophet (SAW) said:

"The world is a prison for the believer and a paradise for the disbeliever." (Sahih Muslim)

When a loved one departs, do not despair. If they died with the testimony of faith, they have returned to Allah, **Al-Ghaffar** (The Forgiving), and His mercy is vast. The Prophet (SAW) said:

"My intercession is guaranteed for whoever says, 'There is no god but Allah,' sincerely from the heart." (Sahih Bukhari)

Consider the story of Abu al-Hasan al-Tihami, who lost his beloved son. In his grief, he wrote an elegy that echoed through the ages, yet in his dream, his son told him:

"I lived among enemies, but now I live near my Lord. What a difference between the two!"

Oh, seeker of truth, know this well;

"What will not walk with you into the grave, release it from your grasp."

For the wise know: this world is but a passing dream, and only love for the Eternal is real.

For there is no goodness in any good that leads to the fire of loss.

And what appears as sorrow, hardship, or bitter trial,

If it guides the soul to the gardens of eternity, can it ever be called evil?

The wise do not measure by the scales of the world,

For gold may turn to dust, and dust may become the foundation of a palace.

O heart, do not be deceived by what pleases the eye;

For true joy is not in what the hand grasps,

But in what the soul embraces when it meets the Divine.

There is no sweetness in honey if it poisons the heart,

And no bitterness in medicine if it leads to healing.

So, turn your face toward the Eternal Light,

And know that whatever brings you closer to Him;

Even if it be wrapped in hardship; is the greatest gift of all.

O grieving soul, your loved one has returned to Allah, **Al-Malik** (The King), and His mercy is greater than your sorrow.

Reflection 7: All Acts of Worship Are Built on Patience.

Fasting, for example, is patience over desires, and Allah, **Al-Shakoor** (The Appreciative), says:

"Every deed of the son of Adam is for him, except fasting. It is for Me, and I will reward it." (Sahih Bukhari)

Hajj is a journey of patience, and its reward is nothing less than Paradise. Allah, **Al-Wahhab** (The Bestower), says:

"And whoever relies upon Allah, then He is sufficient for him." (Quran 65:3)

When the people of Paradise enter, the angels will greet them:

"Peace be upon you for what you patiently endured. And excellent is the final home." (Quran 13:24)

Be patient, O soul, for Allah, **Al-Saboor** (The Patient), has spoken a word of truth:

"Indeed, the patient will be given their reward without account." (Quran 39:10)

On the Day of Resurrection, when the scales are set, the patient will be rewarded beyond measure. They will gaze upon the bounties of Allah, **Al-Kareem** (The Generous), and their hearts will overflow with gratitude. For those who are afflicted, whether by disability, disease, or hardship, know this: Allah, **Al-Raheem** (The Most Merciful), is more compassionate to you than you are to yourself.

Allah, **Al-Hakeem** (The All-Wise), tests you only with what is meant to purify your soul, elevate your rank, and draw you closer to Him. He knows what you do not know, and His wisdom is beyond our comprehension.

O you who are patient, seek help through prayer and patience, for Allah, **Al-Wali** (The Protector), is with the patient. He says:

"O you who have believed, seek help through patience and prayer. Indeed, Allah is with the patient." (Quran 2:153)

When disaster strikes, the patient say:

"Indeed, we belong to Allah, and to Him we shall return." (Quran 2:156)

These are the ones upon whom blessings and mercy descend from their Lord, and they are the rightly guided.

Patience is not merely endurance; it is the art of seeing the Divine Hand in every trial. Like the river that flows tirelessly toward the ocean, the patient soul moves steadily toward Allah, **Al-Wadood** (The Loving).

When the heart is heavy with grief, remember the story of Prophet Ibrahim (AS), who left his wife Hajar and infant son Ismail in the barren desert, trusting in Allah, **Al-Razzaq** (The Provider). Hajar ran between Safa and Marwa, her heart filled with hope, and Allah blessed her with the Zamzam spring, a miracle of His mercy.

O afflicted one, be patient and optimistic, for Allah, **Al-Lateef** (The Subtle), turns hardships into blessings. The Prophet Muhammad (SAW) said:

"How wonderful is the affair of the believer! His affairs are all good, and this is for no one but the believer. If something good happens to him, he is grateful, and that is good for him. If something bad happens to him, he is patient, and that is good for him." (Sahih Muslim)

Reflection 8: Trust in Allah's Plan

O you who are burdened with debt, illness, or disability, know that Allah, **Al-Baseer** (The All-Seeing), is aware of your struggle. The Prophet Ayyub (AS) endured around 18 years of illness, lost his wealth, and buried his children, yet he remained patient, saying:

"Indeed, adversity has touched me, and You are the Most Merciful of the merciful." (Quran 21:83)

O you who feel deprived of love or beauty, remember that Allah, **Al-Jameel** (The Beautiful), created you in the best form.

The Prophet (SAW) said:

"Allah is beautiful and loves beauty." (Sahih Muslim)

O you who are lonely or abandoned, know that Allah, **Al-Wali** (The Protector), is your companion.

He says:

"Do not grieve; indeed, Allah is with us." (Quran 9:40)

Trials are not punishments; they are lessons from Allah, **Al-Aleem** (The All-Knowing).

He says:

"And We will surely test you with something of fear, hunger, loss of wealth, lives, and fruits. But give good tidings to the patient." (Quran 2:155)

Perhaps you hate something, but Allah, **Al-Khabeer** (The All-Aware), places much good in it. Like the story of Musa (AS), who was thrown into the river as a baby, only to be raised in the palace of Pharaoh, the very man who sought to kill him. Allah's plan is perfect, even when we cannot see it.

Trust in Allah, **Al-Wakeel** (The Trustee), and do the necessary means.

The Prophet (SAW) said:

"Tie your camel and trust in Allah." (Sunan At-Tirmidhi)

When you pray Istikhara, say:

"O Allah, I seek Your guidance by Your knowledge, and I seek ability by Your power. If this matter is good for me in my religion, my life, and my hereafter, then decree it for me and make it easy. But if it is bad for me, then turn it away from me and decree for me what is good."

Allah, **Al-Mujeeb** (The Responder), will guide your heart and ease your path.

O soul, do not despair of Allah's mercy. He is **Al-Ghafoor** (The Forgiving) and **Al-Raheem** (The Most Merciful).

He says:

"O My servants who have transgressed against themselves, do not despair of the mercy of Allah. Indeed, Allah forgives all sins. Indeed, it is He who is the Forgiving, the Merciful." (Quran 39:53)

Be patient, for Allah, **Al-Saboor** (The Patient), is with you. Be grateful, for Allah, **Al-Shakoor** (The Appreciative), multiplies your rewards. And be hopeful, for Allah, **Al-Wadood** (The Loving), has prepared for you a home in Paradise, where no eye has seen, no ear has heard, and no heart has imagined its beauty.

May Allah, the Most High, grant us patience, ease our burdens, and make us among those who are pleased with His decree. Ameen.

"Indeed, with hardship comes ease. Indeed, with hardship comes ease." (Quran 94:5-6)

So be still, oh restless soul. The ink of your destiny is not held in your hands, but in the hands of the One who loves you more than you love yourself. You are exactly where you are meant to be. Trust, be patient, and let your heart rest in the hands of **Al-Wahid** (The One).

Reflection 9: Between Fear and Hope

In the heart of every believer, two wings lift the soul toward Allah: **fear** (*khawf*) and **hope** (*rajā'*). These are not contradictions but complements; like the night and day that shape our journey.

Fear, not of despair but of awe,
Like standing by the edge of law.
It guards the heart from slipping down,
Reminds the soul Who owns the crown.

"Indeed, I fear, if I should disobey my Lord, the punishment of a tremendous Day."
(*Qur'an 6:15*)

This fear is light, not shade,
That makes the careless soul afraid.

Hope, like dawn after the storm,
Keeps the wounded spirit warm.
It lifts the eyes to skies so wide,
And says, "With Allah, mercy does abide."

**"Say, O My servants who have transgressed against themselves,
do not despair of the mercy of Allah."**
(*Qur'an 39:53*)

The Prophet Muhammad (*peace be upon him*) said:

**"If the believer knew the punishment of Allah,
he would not feel secure from the Hellfire,
and if he knew the mercy of Allah,
he would not despair of Paradise."**
(*Sahih Muslim, 2755*)

Balance is the path, a bridge so thin,
Too much fear may crush within.
Too much hope? The soul may sleep;

Forgetting promises it must keep.
But **between the two, the heart must soar**,
As ships sail safely between each shore.

Nothing captures this more eloquently than the verse below; let it resonate in your heart, not merely pass through your tongue.

"Indeed, the grip (or punishment) of your Lord is severe."

"Indeed, it is He who originates (creation) and repeats (it)."

"And He is the All-Forgiving, the Most Loving."   Surah Al-Buruj (85:12,13,14)

So fly, O soul, with balanced wings;
Let fear shape and drive your deeds

Guiding you toward righteous leads.

Let hope uplift, never pull you low,

A balanced heart where faith will grow.

A fire that purifies, a breeze that soothes.

Reflection 10: Be a Light in the Darkness

Strive to be among those who bring joy to others, whose lives are a reflection of the mercy of **Ar-Rahman**. Let your heart be a garden of kindness, your hands a river of generosity, and your soul a beacon of light. Avoid the traps of selfishness, fear, and obsession. Trust in the plan of **Al-Aleem** (The All-Knowing), and live a life of purpose and meaning.

May Allah make us and you among those who benefit others and find joy in His mercy.

A Final Whisper to recap the most known names of our Lord

O Lord, **Al-Rahman**, with mercy so wide,
Al-Raheem, whose kindness is our guide.
Al-Malik, the Sovereign, ruling supreme,
Al-Quddus, so Pure, in light we gleam.

Al-Salam, the Source of peace so true,
Al-Mu'min, the Guardian who sees us through.
Al-Muhaymin, the Watchful, ever near,
Al-Aziz, Almighty, instilling no fear.

Al-Jabbar, the Compeller, strong and grand,
Al-Mutakabbir, with honor in hand.
Al-Khaliq, the Creator, shaping all,
Al-Bari', the Evolver, hearing our call.

Al-Musawwir, the Fashioner, designs with grace,
Al-Ghaffar, oft-Forgiving, sins He'll erase.
Al-Qahhar, the Subduer, might beyond sight,
Al-Wahhab, the Giver, with gifts infinite.

Al-Razzaq, the Sustainer, grants what we need,
Al-Fattah, the Opener, paths He'll lead.
Al-'Alim, the All-Knowing, wisdom so vast,
Al-Qabid, the Withholder, trials that pass.

Al-Basit, the Extender, blessings untold,
Al-Khafid, who lowers with justice bold.
Al-Rafi', the Exalter, raising who He wants,
Al-Mu'izz, the Honorer, honor we seek.

Al-Mudhill, the Dishonorer, justice is fair,
Al-Sami', the All-Hearing, answers our prayer.
Al-Basir, the All-Seeing, watching each deed,
Al-Hakam, the Just, fulfilling each need.

Al-Latif, the Subtle, with kindness so pure,
Al-Khabir, All-Aware, whose wisdom is sure.
Al-Halim, the Forbearing, slow to chastise,
Al-'Azim, Most Great, beyond the skies.

Al-Ghaffur, the Forgiver, wipes away blame,
Al-Shakur, Most Appreciative, knows each name.
Al-'Aliyy, Most High, above all ranks,
Al-Kabir, Most Great, to Him our thanks.

Al-Hafiz, the Preserver, guards every soul,
Al-Muqit, the Sustainer, filling each role.
Al-Hasib, the Reckoner, justice He weighs,
Al-Jalil, Most Glorious, beyond our praise.

Al-Karim, Most Generous, grants us light,
Al-Raqib, the Watchful, sees day and night.
Al-Mujib, the Responsive, answers each call,
Al-Wasi', the Vast, embracing all.

Al-Hakim, the Wise, decrees are right,
Al-Wadud, the Loving, hearts shine bright.
Al-Majid, Most Glorious, honor He shows,
Al-Ba'ith, the Resurrector, life bestows.

Al-Shahid, the Witness, truth in His sight,
Al-Haqq, the Absolute, guiding to light.
Al-Wakil, the Trustee, whom we rely,
Al-Qawiyy, the Strong, beyond the sky.

Al-Matin, the Firm, steady and sure,
Al-Waliyy, the Patron, protector so pure.
Al-Hamid, the Praiseworthy, exalted in name,
Al-Muhsi, the Reckoner, counting the same.

Al-Mubdi', the Originator, first in decree,
Al-Mu'id, the Restorer, sets spirits free.
Al-Muhyi, the Giver of life anew,
Al-Mumit, the Creator of death so true.

Al-Hayy, the Ever-Living, never shall fade,
Al-Qayyum, the Sustainer, whom none evade.
Al-Wajid, the Finder, none can conceal,
Al-Majid, Most Glorious, His love is real.

Al-Wahid, the One, none can compare,
Al-Ahad, the Indivisible, beyond all air.
Al-Samad, the Eternal, needs none at all,
Al-Qadir, the Omnipotent, answering the call.

Al-Muqtadir, Creator of fate and time,
Al-Muqaddim, the Expediter, order sublime.
Al-Mu'akhkhir, the Delayer, knows when and why,
Al-Awwal, the First, beyond the sky.

Al-Akhir, the Last, whom time obeys,
Al-Zahir, the Manifest, His light displays.
Al-Batin, the Hidden, beyond our mind,
Al-Wali, the Sole Governor, just and kind.

Al-Muta'ali, the Self-Exalted, high above,
Al-Barr, the Source of Good, endless love.
Al-Tawwab, the Accepter of our plea,
Al-Muntaqim, the Avenger, firm decree.

Al-'Afuww, Most Pardoning, erasing the past,
Al-Ra'uf, Most Kind, His mercy is vast.
Malik-ul-Mulk, Master of all domain,
Dhul-Jalali Wal-Ikram, glory remains.

Al-Muqsit, the Just, fairness prevails,
Al-Jami', the Gatherer, truth He unveils.
Al-Ghaniyy, the Self-Sufficient, needing none,
Al-Mughni, the Enricher, blessings are spun.

Al-Mani', the Withholder, protecting from harm,
Al-Darr, the Distresser, testing with charm.
Al-Nafi', the Benefactor, kindness extends,
Al-Nur, the Light, our darkness He mends.

Al-Hadi, the Guide, shows us the way,
Al-Badi', the Incomparable, none can sway.
Al-Baqi, the Ever-Surviving, never to end,
Al-Warith, the Inheritor, to whom all ascend.

Al-Rashid, the Guide, with wisdom profound,
Al-Sabur, the Patient, mercy unbound.
Exalted are You, O Lord Most High,
To You we turn, to You we cry.

O Lord, the whisper of my soul calls Your names,
The One beyond kings, beyond all acclaim.
More merciful than a mother's embrace,
More generous than the endless grace.

You give without asking, You bless without bound,
No partner have You, no limit be found.
All fades but You, the Eternal Light,
No step is taken but by Your might.

Secrets dissolve in the depth of Your wise,
Hearts unfold in the warmth of Your mercy.
You weave the thread of what's pure and true,
And shield from paths that darken the view.

The law, the life, the love, the decree,
All flows from You like the boundless sea.
I am but dust, yet Yours to mold,
You are the refuge, the shelter, the hold.

By the weight of truth, by mercy untold,
I ask but one gift, more precious than gold:
When dawn awakens that fateful day,
Let fire not take me; guide me Your way.

O soul, let not the Names of Allah remain ink upon a page or echoes in the air. Let them settle into your heart, bloom in your actions, and shine through your being. The Beloved calls; will you not answer?

The Book Cover

This cover is a profound visual metaphor, crafted to embody the essence of Tawhid; the oneness of Allah; and the richness of His Divine Names. Shaped in the form of the number "1," the design speaks to the foundational Islamic truth: There is no deity but Allah. This singular form is not only symbolic but purposeful, representing unity amidst diversity; each Name of Allah unique, yet all belonging to the One.

The typography within the "1" is more than decoration; it is data, devotion, and design fused into one. The varying sizes of the Divine Names are not random but intentional: the larger the name, the more frequently it appears in the Qur'an. This proportional representation offers a subtle, scholarly insight; honoring the rhythm and emphasis found in the sacred text itself. Names like The All-Knowing, The Almighty, and The Most Gracious take visual precedence, reminding us of their central role in divine revelation and human reflection.

The composition flows upward, subtly guiding the eye and spirit toward ascension; symbolizing that the more we know Allah through His names, the more our souls rise in nearness to Him. The design is at once personal and universal; it invites every viewer into a journey of remembrance (dhikr), knowledge, and connection.

Acknowledgments

To Allah belongs every thread of praise, for without His mercy, my steps would falter, my words would scatter like dust in a restless wind. Every spark of insight, every syllable formed, every thought stitched with purpose; is but a glimpse of His boundless wisdom. It is He who guides the pen, who breathes clarity into the mind, for not a leaf turns, nor a heart beats, save by His will alone.

Endless gratitude I send to the beloved Messenger, Muhammad (peace and blessings be upon him), the mercy gifted to all of creation, whose light stretches across the ages, steadying every step I take.

Without the mercy of Allah, and without the enduring light of His Prophet, this path would be barren, and this effort but an empty shell. May every word in this work rise as a humble offering, a flicker of gratitude for the mercy poured upon me. And may Allah, Most High, continue to bless and guide us all upon the straight path, as He once blessed those noble ones who walked it before us.

I also extend acknowledgment to the silent hands of technology, especially the aid of AI tools, which served quietly yet faithfully through the stages of this journey.

References

Al-Bukhari, M. I. (n.d.). *Sahih al-Bukhari* (M. Muhsin Khan, Trans.). Dar-us-Salam Publications. (Original work compiled ca. 846 CE).

Al-Bahli, A. (2020). Abd Rahman Al-Bahli; Lecture series.

Al-Suwaidan, T. (2024). Allah (SWT) in the Holy Quran: The names and attributes of Allah; *Lecture series.*

Ezz, Ashi. (2024). *Muhammad: Lasting Resilience Model.* [Available on Amazon: https://a.co/d/e7hR0rB]. ISBN: 978-1-0670358-3-9.

Ezz, Ashi (2024). *Ashrafiyah hymn book* [Kindle edition]. Amazon Digital Services. https://www.amazon.com

The Quran. (n.d.). The Noble Quran in the English Language (Taqi-ud-Din al-Hilali & Muhammad Muhsin Khan, Trans.). King Fahd Complex for the Printing of the Holy Quran. (Original work published ca. 610–632 CE).

Muslim ibn al-Hajjaj. (n.d.). Sahih Muslim. Darussalam Publishers.

Ibn Majah, M. (n.d.). Sunan Ibn Majah. Darussalam Publishers.

Ibn Kathir, I. (n.d.). Tafsir Ibn Kathir. Darussalam Publishers.

Ibn Baz, A. A. (n.d.). Majmoo' Fatawa wa Maqalat Mutanawwi'ah (Collected Fatwas and Various Articles). Riyadh: Presidency of Islamic Research, Ifta, Call and Guidance.

Ibn Uthaymeen, M. S. (n.d.). *Majmoo' Fatawa wa Rasa'il* (Collected Fatwas and Letters). Riyadh: Dar Ath-Thurayya.

About the Author

Dr. Ashi Ezz is an expert in organizational transformation, with a doctorate specializing in risk management. Passionate about inspiring positive change. Dr. Ashi Ezz is a leading resilience strategist and author of transformative models such as CITF, MLRM, and AQRM. Dr. Ashi is dedicated to mentoring and coaching individuals and organizations towards better, more balanced lives. With a wealth of knowledge gained from years of practical experience, engaging with experts, and an insatiable appetite for continuous learning, Dr. Ashi is committed to empowering others to shape successful enterprises and fulfilling personal lives.

www.ingramcontent.com/pod-product-compliance
Lightning Source LLC
Chambersburg PA
CBHW030335010526
44119CB00047B/506